What is Lioness?

No longer are we just small women at home, we are providers, we are mothers, we are multitaskers, we are lionesses. We have been waiting for our time.

This heart warming and inspiring book written by ladies who found themselves wanting to change their lives after having children, to be more flexible and fit in more with mum life. Many found it stressful returning to work and trying to juggle their careers and motherhood others found immense guilt not being home more. Some ladies felt that they lost themselves and are trying to regain their own independence and personality after giving birth. They found their priorities were to be home more so quit their job but needed to provide financially for their family or felt there was no progression in their job and wanted so much which leads to do we work to live or live to work?

This book brings out the creativity and resourcefulness of womankind with ladies finding gaps in the market for their product/service but still fitted with being a mum. These ladies have overcome adversities in their life from fibromyalgia, cancer, abuse, anxiety and depression plus hard times financially with hitting rock bottom and sofa-surfing.

This book was written to encourage ladies to start their own career in self-employment and give you the encouragement and support you need to take the leap of faith. Many ladies in this book are coaches and their passion is to support you.

Towards the back of the book you will find some business worksheets and advice for you to start your own journey.

Join our community: facebook.com/groups/lionesspridegroup

A huge thank you to Cynthia Stevens for proof reading this book.

The Time is Now. We are all Lionesses.

Contents

1. Jane - Louise Pattison - The Photo Lady
2. Vicky Fox - I'm Virtually Here!
3. Mandy Worsley - Forever Mummy
4. Elise Challis - Refuelled, Relaunched.
5. Laura Malcolm - Nuttall - The Journey Back To Myself
6. Georgina Tang - Rising Like A Phoenix
7. Francesca Manca - Big Shoes To Fill, My Way
8. Danielle Hobson - 100% Unemployable
9. Andrea Binks - Life is a Stage
10. Sophie Jones - Glitter is Life!
11. Edwina Clark - From Rock Bottom to Rocking it
12. Sammie Byrne - Unstoppable Introvert
13. Lisa Haythorne - It Just Makes Scents
14. Louisa Herridge - Learning To Bloom
15. Sally Ashkenazi - Signed, Sealed, Delivered
16. Lisa Betsworth - More Than Meets The Eye
17. Kirsty Gibbons - It All Turned Out Different
18. Natalie Reeves Billing - The Girl From The Dingle
19. Fiona Wallace - This Is Me
20. Liz Johnson - The Stay At Home Mum
21. Becca Bryant - There is Life After Childhood Sexual Abuse
22. Antonia Gough - Just Start Somewhere
23. Victoria Rothwell - Cocktails, Children and Cleaning!

"And if the end result is that someone, somewhere winds up believing they can do something out of the ordinary, well, then you've really made it."

ANGELA AHRENDTS

Chapter 1

"The Photo Lady"

Jane - Louise Pattison

"More Than Just A Photographer" covering Chesterfield and surrounding areas providing affordable, professional and fun photography.
Award winning family and wedding photography.

www.janelouisephotography.co.uk
Facebook: @janelouisephotographyuk
Instagram: @janelouisephotographyuk @janelouisephotographyweddings

Her other passion is helping ladies to feel more confident and love the skin they are in. She is passionate about helping ladies to self love and have a safe space to rant and let it all out.

Facebook Group: The Better You Project
Facebook : @bloominggorgeousuk
Instagram: @bloominggorgeousuk

So this book starts with me - Jane. I am the lady who created Lioness to help other ladies start their business and help you avoid the pitfalls I faced. Plus lots of advice of what I have learnt over the years. So let's get into my story.

I am a full time professional photographer and I absolutely love what I do! I fell into photography when my twin girls were two and I was looking at a way to make some money. My grandmother purchased me my first DSLR and I captured some photographs of my girls. I then completed many online courses to understand how to use my camera and how to take professional photographs. I realised there was a gap in the market for affordable professional photography, I had only had one mini session of my girls taken at this point which was incredibly expensive and the photographs were not that great. This was a pop-up event at the local children's centre where you go to get your babies weighed. Previous to this I did plan on setting up selling clothes and purchased some from China but this was an oversaturated market. I then created my own designs and contacted factories who could produce them but luckily I did some market research first. The market research showed that people wanted cheap clothing and for what I could have them created the profit margin was too small. So photography being the new project I contacted a local photographer and he provided me with loads of advice and support which was great. It was lovely to have someone you can bounce off which questions and not feel silly for asking them. That is one of the reasons I started Lioness was so ladies had a safe space to ask questions and bounce ideas around. This was September - December 2016 when I decided to be a photographer. Like my previous experience at the playgroup I realised being at places customers are was easier for the customers and I could keep my costs down.

So I set out to be a mobile photographer, after going to the job centre and explaining I wanted to be self - employed they led me to the Princes Trust. When I signed up I thought it was a course for a few days so I signed all the paperwork and looked forward to a change of scenery. We are now in April 2017 and I registered the business and completed the few day courses to be told I have to go to Nottingham for an evening to complete the course. I also had been assigned a mentor, I thought this was great until I met him and within two meetings realised he had NO idea what I did and my clientele. I was also rather excited about a local contract with a company I had which he pointed out they were just using me which really annoyed me. Yes they were receiving affordable photographs but this was a huge deal for me and I was so proud to have the contract. Plus the contract was worth a lot of money to me and I enjoyed the job. After two meetings he quit being a mentor and I was reassigned a really lovely lady. This lady understood me and my business and she always had great advice and things I never thought about. I really enjoyed my time meeting her, she gave me a great ego boost and her ideas from the outside were great and implemented. I will come back to her shortly.

So the plan was with having no studio my prices could be kept low and I went to playgroups with a two light set up and vinyl backdrop and a few props. My friend runs the local playgroup we used to go to so she let me go there and I contacted several others. I also contacted play centres and farm parks and everywhere local that had child visitors and I offered them a commission for allowing me to be there. I think this is important when you are contacting somewhere wanting something make it clear what they are getting out of it. One of the places I contacted as a second-hand children's clothes and toy store which I went to July 2017. This was my first ever shoot and I was shaking a complete nervous wreck. Looking at those photographs now I may cringe but I should be proud and I left that day feeling elated. I had three customers at £15 each and I was so so happy walking away with my £45. The shop wanted to book some more dates in for Halloween and Christmas and towards the end of the year. They contacted me letting me know they were expanding the shop and would I like a permanent "studio" within it. I couldn't believe it and when I met they said how much a month and I was worried I wouldn't be able to make enough to cover the rent. It was an opportunity I could not turn down so I HAD to make it work. This started January 2018 and I was there until November 30th 2018.

My own little space was amazing, I was so proud of it, I would tell you the measurements but I am really rubbish at measurements it was around the size of a square living room. My husband wallpapered the wall, we fixed my backdrops on and this was the real start of me getting into photography. I didn't have any privacy but it was usually quiet in the area I was in so it felt very much mine. A lot happened whilst at the that studio which I won't get into but it made me realise that not everyone is your friend. Some people are only your friend while they are getting something out of it. It is something you need to be very aware of when in business. Especially if you are soft like me, be aware people will take advantage of this for their own gains. When you go into business you are going to meet a lot of new people and it's important to sift out the snakes and the genuine amazing people who will change your life. This summer also saw me waste a lot of time at places where my ideal clientele wasn't - I got it VERY wrong and spent money on tables at fairs etc and more importantly my time. I will talk a lot about finding your ideal clientele and that is so you don't make the mistake I did here. I also got pressure into financing and signing up to something I didn't want to which was no good for my business. Another lesson is if it's a financial decision always give yourself time to sleep on it, I was ambushed unfortunately!

I applied for the Derbyshire Times Awards 2018 under four categories and my mentor helped write me a piece to support my application. I did not win but I got a commended award for my hard work which I am incredibly proud of. I applied for the Derbyshire Times Awards 2019 and won the Innovation Award for my affordable friendly approach to photography. I am incredibly proud of these awards as it feels recognition for the hours I spend everyday working on my business. Recognition from other peers is an amazing feeling and I highly recommend applying for local awards in your area. Also keep studying as I completed a newborn and maternity in person course for the day where I learnt so much and this gave me the knowledge to branch into newborn and maternity and branched out to more I feel I can do. December 2018 saw me photograph my first ever wedding as a friend encouraged me to do it after I said I couldn't. I was a nervous wreck on the day and the videographer took me under his wing and guided me all day. Those photographs are some of the best I have taken and one won an award with the guild of photographers. I really enjoyed and loved doing this so although I was nervous I LOVE doing weddings so pushing myself out of my comfort zone is the only way forward.

During the summer of 2018 I made a new friend who also wanted their own commercial space and as things went downhill at my old studio we looked for a new one. November 30th 2018 we signed for where my studio is now. I arranged for a removal van early morning before they opened and got all my stuff out and pushed the keys through the letterbox. A huge weight felt like it had been lifted as things had become very toxic at the old studio. I did a live video to show the new studio and although this was supposed to be one of the happiest days I was sat crying. The people from the old studio were commenting to say they were going to visit who I was subletting to and it felt like I had not escaped it. My husband does not get involved in my business or personal friendships but this was the one time he stepped in and spoke to those people. It worked the trick and I could finally move on.

Me and the lady I sublet to had a great time at the new studio, I sublet to her so the building was my responsibility and she had a section for what she wanted to do. This worked really well up until Covid happened which led to her having to leave the studio due to financial issues. I have now reopened the studio on both sides which makes life a lot easier for me having more space. Rather than me having to do a set up, quickly put it away and do another whilst the customer waits I have "zones" at the studio for different things. When I took the tenancy on I always made sure I could afford it outright just in case a situation like this happened. I absolutely love my studio, the location, the area, the local people and everything. It really does feel like it was destined to be.

A little bit more about me, I remember being sixteen at school and connexions came into school and they were to help you find your future career. They asked questions like "Do you want to work inside? Or outside?" I remember saying outside when its sunny and inside when it is not. I can't remember what they said my dream job was, that was the only thing I remember. I have always been into taking photographs but I'm not someone who poses for selfies regularly. I had worked in pubs previous to this and I loved talking to people and getting to know people. The hours are unsociable around family life and the pay isn't great so I really didn't want to go back to that. I do feel I have found my true calling in life being a photographer. I honestly wake up everyday and love my job and my reviews and customers can echo this. I think once you fall out of love with a job you need to move onto something else. The passion is what keeps you fuelled.

I have faced many challenges which have mainly been due to people and friendships but you do overcome them. Once you have in sight what you want you make sure nothing gets in the way. My business is to provide for my family and nothing is more important that my family. If someone is blocking this then I will remove them from my life because you don't need people like that. Lioness is to help ladies get straight on that ladder and boss their business with everything I have taken three years to learn. From social media to marketing and branding and mindset. Mindset is the most important thing, being self-employed has many perks but it can be very time consuming. Although you set your own hours I can be messaging customers 6am and 12pm, I don't have a "day off" as I am constantly doing something business related. This is my choice of course but you will find most self-employed people are of this mindset. Being a good business owner in today's world is all about networking and connecting with others. My free Facebook group Lioness Pride: Helping ladies to launch and grow their business is to help ladies connect and support one another.

As well as being a photographer I have a few other side businesses, one being Lioness which I have mentioned and of course this book is linked to. I have a very supportive nature and help run a local business networking groups for mothers alongside other amazing ladies. Lioness is a free Facebook community and amazing affordable courses to help ladies with their businesses. I am also an ambassador of a MLM company of which I am incredibly passionate about. I am reaching a large milestone and its time to start looking after my skin and body. I have some amazing ladies in my team and would love to help more ladies create extra income and make friends. I have created a Facebook group for my journey and for other ladies to make pledges. Pledges to be better versions of themselves whether it be weight loss, weight gain, mindset changes, mental health support or any issues to be a better version of themselves. (The Better You Project). Too many times ladies put themselves last especially when they become mothers (I am guilty of this) so I like the idea of setting some time aside to pamper yourself and look after you - because you are so important.

My background is working in pubs and I have a degree in Psychology and Counselling and studied a Masters in Applied Animal Behaviour and Training. I find the skills I learnt from both of these have been really helpful with my every day life and career. Being able to read and deal with clients is an important part of my job. I make clients feel comfortable and at ease and they enjoy coming for shoots. Being good at my job is a skill I am working on but the important part is customer service which I have learnt. I have also upgraded my camera twice during the last few years and equipment, it's important to grow as a business and as a person. Having my twin girls and becoming a mother provided me with the patience and understanding on children. Everything that has happened in my life I have gained skills and knowledge and apply them every day.

So thats a bit about me, I hope you enjoy this book learning about the other amazing ladies. I searched for ladies from different backgrounds and different stories and businesses so you can see that anyone can do this if they really want to. I hope you feel inspired.

> The most successful entrepreneurs I know are optimistic. It's part of the job description."

CATERINA FAKE

Chapter 2

I'm Virtually Here!

Vicky Fox

Fox Business Support

Providing freelance virtual admin support using traditional values

www.foxbusinesssupport.co.uk

Facebook: @foxbusinesssupport
Twitter: @foxsupport1

I have always been a 'doer' with no patience for anything monotonous and boring. High energy but not particularly creative, always needed direction.

At school I was fairly bright but found it difficult to apply myself, especially with subjects that didn't interest me. I liked to see a result and purpose for doing something. I had many part-time jobs since the age of 13 as I've always had a strong work ethic and always loved earning my own money.

After leaving school and not really knowing which direction to take as anything I found interesting or had a passion for was disapproved of as a career being told "you don't want to mix your hobby with your job as you'll end up resenting it". I tell my children the exact opposite that if you can find a job that you enjoy and feels like a hobby at the same time then go for it! Like so many before me have said, you are at work for a long time so why not do something that you enjoy!? As I didn't have much idea of what I wanted to do as I wasn't that much good at anything other than sport, it was suggested I go to college to do a secretarial course, which I did but then quickly moved to do a business and finance course for more of a challenge.

After leaving college with a distinction I gained a place at university but again wasn't given much guidance or advice so ended up on a business and quality management course. It was far too academic for me with too much theory. I'm also a real home bird and got incredibly homesick.

I finished and passed my first year, but then left to find work as at that time I couldn't see the value in staying on a course which would take me on a career path that I didn't really want to be on. At this point I was called a fool for not finishing University, but I haven't lived to regret it… yet!

So, I went to work and started in business admin and eventually gained five promotions in five years. I then had my two children within twelve months of returning to work after each was six months old. I was always very loyal to my employer and I was conscious that it was costing them money whenever I was off, even though it was local government. On returning to work I continued to apply myself, worked hard and tried to balance being a mum and having a career. It worked ok for another eight years and then things started to change. My husband had the opportunity to take a promotion at work which would mean being away from home during the week. Even before he worked away, he wasn't in a position to help with childcare at all. I always found childcare difficult as the children never liked nursery or childminders and I was always the one who had to leave for sickness, injury etc etc. I never resented the children, but I found I was meeting myself coming backwards all the time. I had one particular bust up with a boss when they accused me of making up childcare issues to get out of doing a course. This enraged me as I had always done everything I could to maintain the upmost level of professionalism whilst also being a mum. I even worked at an event once whilst my daughter had chicken pox. On another occasion I asked my mum to take my son for a routine eye test to then find out he needed glasses. I was really upset that I hadn't been there to take on board all of the information we were given about the next steps. Something quite minor, but nevertheless important. I could never forgive my line manager for that accusation so looked to move to another position as soon as possible as I took it very personally. After a year that opportunity came. I was very under qualified for the position, but they seemed to like me, and we thought we could make it work. A few months into my new position my mother-in-law hurt her knee when she was due to pick the children up from school for me… this again caused a childcare issue with my current line manager (I'd only had one other instance of needing to pick up a sick child from school – by the way, both times my line managers were male with no childcare responsibilities themselves!). Once again, I was devastated. I never had time off sick, always worked until the job was done but for what? I have never been able to cope well if I thought that I was letting people down and at this point I just felt like I was letting everyone down all the time. I was getting paid well for a job I didn't know how to do and with no leadership or guidance even with me actively seeking it.

Reading a magazine, I came across an article based on side hussles and one of those featured a Virtual Assistant. I kept the article for a long time and wish to this day that I still had a copy. When the shit finally hit the fan at the Local Authority (LA) where I had worked for sixteen years, I referred back to the article and started to research this opportunity in more detail as I thought it would be viable option to finally get out of the situation I was in. After many hours of research, I started to put a plan into action including an exit strategy. I had only been in my latest position at the LA for eight months when I handed in my notice. As a favour, my line manager asked me to stay part time to see the Department through a re-organisation, which I did only for another manager to think I was trying to play the system. There was definitely a culture of mistrust amongst top management… probably through their own making! There was no trust at all and I honestly think that my then line manager was making out that I was calling the shots and not actually staying on as the favour that he had pitched it to me as. As soon as I had enough clients, I handed my notice in with no re-negotiations and no regrets… I have never looked back!

I have been my own boss now for over three years and I LOVE IT! I have since never had an issue with childcare and no one making me feel like a failure (only myself when I put pressure on!). I will never again have to work for someone I do not respect or take a position that I am not able to do just to escape from another. I earn my own money and I have done it all myself! Don't get me wrong, it's bloody hard work, but totally worth it!!!

Growth and comfort do not coexist."

GINNI ROMETTY

Chapter 3

forever Mummy

Mandy Worsley

Mandy is a mum to two amazing children through adoption and foster mummy for past two years. She left the NHS after 26 years to follow her dream to build her own home for her family and open it as a retreat for adoptive families and a hub for local people to come and experience calm on the farm.

www.chethamfarmretreat.com

Instagram: @chethamfarmretreat

Hi, my name is Mandy I am forty-eight years old and I grew up as an only child in a small village in Lancashire. I had a happy childhood and an uneventful school life. I had always loved children and longed for my mum to have a baby sibling for me, which never happened but later in life I did meet my two half sisters who are just my sisters now and I love them dearly. That love of children has been a theme throughout my life and all my work has revolved around that and I used to feel hard done to that I was unable to give birth, I won't say I couldn't have my own children because the children I have are my own, and I could not love them anymore than if they had been born to me and I truly believe that my struggles in life lead me to just exactly where I am needed to be and following the path I need to be on and to open my heart up to so many children in my life.

After leaving sixth form and applying to nursing college I had a gap year where I worked as a nanny for two local families before moving to Leeds to train as a Children's Nurse in the NHS where I worked for over twenty-six years. I worked in two large children's hospitals, in the community, in school health and also as a nurse tutor in practice linked to a large university. I loved my job and seeing the difference I could make to children and families lives made each day worthwhile, but sadly I felt I had to leave in 2016 due to the culture of bullying in the workplace which lead me to be on the verge of a nervous breakdown. I had gained six stone in weight, had high blood pressure, daily headaches and a diagnosis of very severe sleep apnoea. I was depressed and unhappy and needed to make some big changes in my life.

During this time also I had gone through some major trauma in my quest to be a mummy, which was my life-long wish, but it was not to be an easy road with six rounds of IVF which left me mentally, physically and financially broken, all the while showing up for work as a happy hardworking nurse giving love and care to other people's children while inside my heart was broken. One of the most difficult moments was getting a positive test but finding out at eight weeks that my baby had stopped growing and having to wait all over Christmas and new year to be taken into hospital for a procedure to remove the foetus, which in the end I miscarried naturally- a day I will never forget…….. but at the same time this happened my son whom I adopted at the age of nine months was conceived and my journey to me being his mummy began, I truly believe fate stepped in and gave me the children who needed all this love inside me that I had to give.

He was born shortly after the baby I lost would have been born and was given up for adoption. He was the best thing that ever happened to me and the day he came home and made me a mummy is a special day in our house that we have celebrated every year for the past fifteen years, his gotcha day, he loves it as its like a second birthday with a family meal out with a friend invited to mark the day we became a family. We do the same for my daughter who made us complete as a family of four a couple of years later.

In 2016 when I took redundancy I needed to make some changes to my health and I began to feel hopeful for our future again,I wanted life to be better to be a good mum and not just someone who worked hard but was stressed and unhappy and ill. As a family we had a vision and a dream to build our own house on our family farm. Between 2013-2015 the plans for the house developed from just a family home into a business venture also, as this is what the council wanted for us to be able to go ahead with the build, so the idea of Chetham Farm Retreat was born.

It was not an easy road as we are in a green belt area, so we dug deep and fought hard to make our paper dreams become a reality. We had many planning meeting, local council meeting, parish council meeting and it was another test of my strength.

The original idea was for a home with a Bed and Breakfast business attached, but if I'm honest this didn't really sing to me, but as I lay there one night on the farm in the caravan we had moved into with the kids, two cats and a guinea pig it came to me. Why not make it a place for adopted or foster families to come and stay, where they could relax and bond and take time out to just be a family. I had just taken redundancy from my job in the NHS after twenty-six years and I was looking for something I could retrain in and I came across a programme called Relax Kids. This is a programme that helps children and adults to learn relaxation techniques through movement of the body, yoga, massage, mindfulness and meditation. Following my training in 2017 I started working freelance with adoptive families, foster families and schools to offer emotional health and well-being. I drew on my twenty-six year's experience as a paediatric nurse working in mental health, my relax kids training and other trainings I have taken over the past few years including positive touch through story massage to enhance my skills and knowledge. I also worked very closely with my local authority talking to prospective adopters and was also an active panel member for an adoption charity in Manchester.

All the while the retreat was taking shape and being built. After seventeen months of caravan living, we were finally able to move into half the house and get the B&B up and running, although we were also staying in the guest bedrooms so if we had a booking we all had to pile into one room! The retreat has also evolved from just being a B&B to becoming a holistic hub where we run yoga, meditation and workshops and relax kids and just relax sessions for all aspects of emotional health and well-being.

My vision of working with adoptive families from the retreat and offering therapeutic support is still an ongoing project. We have been contacted by Cambridge LA who want to send a few families to us, and describe the package of support we offer as unique and not on offer anywhere else in the UK, this is amazing that we have been recognised as providing a service that is needed, but this in itself brings its own challenges as we really hoped that these breaks could be funded by the Adoption Support Fund (ASF) but so far this had not been possible.

I believe that is because we are breaking the mould, stepping outside of the traditional and offering something bespoke, unique and innovative so I just see this as another challenge we have to face and we won't give up on dream to help and support adoptive families. We have been successful in getting relax kids funded for this family with a local coach in that area. We have worked with many outside of the retreat setting and also had self-funded families come and stay and will keep on pushing to be recognised by the adoption support fund, which will then make our service accessible to all families in need of this vital work. We believed 2020 was the year that Chetham farm retreat will become the centre of support for many families in need.

Then Covid 19 hit us and we had to close the doors on our retreat, our dream and what was the roof over our head. This past five months have been hard, with lots of phone calls to mortgage lenders, banks, the local council etc and surviving on the bare minimum and having to claim benefits just to put food on the table. But every cloud has a silver lining and for me this has come in the form for of online work for adoptive families delivering the relax kids programme which has been funded by the Adoption Support fund! This gives me great hope that my foot is firmly wedged in the door now to make my offer of short breaks (once we are able to open) to adoptive families and for them to be able to get funding for that.

Each step of my life has taught me to be strong, resilient but mostly to have a dream and a vision so strong that no matter what is put in your way, how winding the road maybe, never give up and take each stone on your path and use it to build a mountain, because the view from the top is stunning.

"Don't waste a single second. Just move forward as fast as you can, and go for it."

REBECCA WOODCOCK

Chapter 4

Refuelled, Relaunched.

Elise Challis

Supporting people to feel healthier and happier; learning new strategies which help to achieve goals, recapture sparkle and sustain positive changes. Also - sharing holistic, natural approaches to help ditch issues such as bloating, exhaustion or weight problems.

Learning to love 'the skin we are in' while supporting each other in building self esteem and positive wellbeing.

Ask her about her VIP Home From Home Retreat - bringing the retreat to you in the comfort of your own home.

Facebook: @HolisticHealthyLivingWithElise
Instagram: @standuptofibro

My Journey of Ups, Downs and Turnarounds.

I start my story back when I was just a little girl. Probably around the time I was still playing in front of the house after school, collecting furbies and obsessed with Blue Peter. I grew up living with my mum and my older sister Zoe, who was just over two years older than me. Whilst my mum was bringing us up on her own, she always made sure we had everything we needed, and she brought us up with strong family values. I remember watching an NSPCC advert one day and saying to my mum "I want to help children like that". I can't have been that old myself, but already I was setting the foundations for wanting to be in a profession where I could help others.

I always grew up with strong work ethics being portrayed to me. My dad owned his own business and I remember him travelling all over the place on his own, sometimes driving for hours to see just one customer. He would leave for work at four/five am to beat the traffic and sleep in his car or drive through the night to places far away. My dad's company was providing people with reverse osmosis systems, which purified their water. Also both my mum and dad ran an organic food delivery service.

I can remember back to when I was little and my mum was completing a distant learning course, she would spend evenings reading, studying and completing work. On my first day of primary school she started a new job and went on to manage the charity during my school life. She was working in a setting that supported people with mental health problems, so I would often get involved in the community events and help out with things such as flower arranging, music events or just simply coffee and cake drop ins. I really enjoyed this, as it was my first experience of working in a voluntary setting for a charity that had an incredible impact on people's lives.

When it came to my own school life experience, I was the daughter that was a bit slower at learning things. I would study so hard, and revise for exams, take ages to complete coursework and projects and come out with a middle ground grade. My sister was the brainy one who would revise last minute, remember all the capitals of countries, do everything the night before and get graded an A*. Unfair I hear you say, you'd be right, but it never stopped me from trying. If anything, I think it spurred me on more, because I thought she must have been revising or learning in secret. It taught me resilience as well.

In lessons I would always be the geeky student that had all the high lighters, new pencil case, new notebook, sticky notes everywhere and basically write word for word what was being taught to me. All in the hope that I would remember things better.

I was a really sporty child and inherited this from my dad. He completed numerous marathons whilst I was growing up and would encourage my sporting abilities. I seemed to outperform my sister in the sporting abilities which was something I was very proud of. I remember thinking she got the brains and I got the sporting talents. I trained hard and represented my county in running, hockey, netball and was seeded number one in Tennis for a couple of years. I took my sport really seriously and perhaps focussed more on this because I was good at, unlike my academic studies. This was merely reinforced by the fact I was in the bottom maths class and often felt like I was being left behind by the other students. So, although I knew I wanted to help people when I was older, I wasn't sure what this would look like in terms of a profession, as I wasn't sure I would achieve much from a grades perspective.

When I turned fourteen I unfortunately contracted E.coli poisoning whilst I was away on holiday in Cyprus with my dad and sister. After one or two days of the holiday I remember feeling unwell, I felt sick, faint and very tired. My dad thought I had sun stroke for the whole holiday. What I hadn't told anyone was that I was bleeding from multiple places and that I couldn't keep even water down. The main memory I have of this holiday was that our flight was delayed by five hours. I took refuge in the toilet without either my sister or dad knowing how seriously unwell I felt. I was embarrassed. No fourteen year old wants to tell their dad about bleeding from their bottom or in their vomit. At one point it all became too much, I had pushed the toilet cubicle door open and asked a lady to help find my sister. I was naked laying on the floor feeling very weak, I remember praying to survive I felt so poorly. I spent many weeks in hospital afterwards as it had caused quite a lot of damage. All from an undercooked beef burger on holiday!!! Little did I know this would be the beginning of my journey of chronic illness.

This hugely effected my sporting abilities as I was left with health complications, mostly around my digestion system at this stage. So, from the age of fourteen I was in and out of hospital, tests after tests, canulas, needles, examinations, scans, internal cameras and constant pulling around. I was also sick so much that it did a lot of damage to my teeth, so I now have a phobia of the dentist because of the amount of work that was needed doing. I managed to get through school with fairly decent grades, thanks to extra lessons my mum paid for and a HUGE amount of work on my behalf. But I did it, and that was an achievement in itself, because when you're unwell everything seems so much harder.

I had by this point decided that I wanted to be a Social Worker, so I needed some work experience to show that I was the right person for this role and to be able to start the degree. I volunteered for Victim Support, Cruse Bereavement and Mencap. Alongside this I was working in a fruit and veg shop, waitressing and doing direct door to door sales to try and pay my rent as I moved out at eighteen years old. I was always a very resourceful person as I felt like I was a bit of a fighter due to ill health and as I said at the beginning of my story I was resilient from a young age. I battled wanting to do things, but my body not allowing me to and this not only annoyed me, but made me want to do things even more.

In my final year at University my body tried stopping me once more. I developed ulcers and linears in my bowel and I was in excruciating pain. I was put on a high number of steroids and pain relief. I refused to let this stop me from completing three years of seriously hard work. I never thought I would be able to get a degree, so my bowel certainly wasn't going to stop me now. Through gritted teeth I was determined to get a pass which I did! With a great big moon face from the steroids I finally got my graduation pictures that everyone dreams of. This was the gateway for me to start my dream of being a Social Worker and finally being able to help disadvantaged children.

Nine years in a front-line Child Protection team became my second home. I spent many evenings working late in the office, in a police station, hospital CP suite or in a court room. I even went in to work on my days off or over the Christmas period. I didn't have children of my own and was an unattached professional female, so my work became my life and my identity. Being shouted at, chased, threatened became the norm, and putting my work before my own health and wellbeing sadly became the reality. In 2015 work hit me in ways I never thought possible. For some reason I was no longer able to suppress my feelings or emotions. I had tried to bury how I was feeling and internalise things as I had managed to do so well for the years prior to this. However, this time, my body was not taking it anymore. I went from lifting weights and boxing five times a week, to not even be able to hold my phone. I'd wake up in the mornings feeling like I had been run over by a bus and drugged. No amount of sleep was enough and the pain was spreading through my body more and more each day. I was later diagnosed with Fibromyalgia and Raynaud's Syndrome.

Learning to juggle chronic illness and leading a normal working life is challenging at the best of times. Just as you feel like you have your symptoms under control something as simple as a change in the weather, stress in your life, or poor sleep can turn your symptoms on their head. I managed to find ways of keeping my fibromyalgia under control, enough to allow me to continue enjoying my work and living a relatively normal life. However at the age of thirty I realised that my work was literally my life, and that it was unbalanced in terms of how I was looking after myself both physically and emotionally.

I met my husband in the February 2017. After a very tricky relationship with my ex I had sworn myself off any other relationships. However I knew as soon as I met him he was the one. As corny as that sounds, it's true. I hadn't wanted to find someone at that stage and it's like the universe was putting things in my way that I needed in my life. It's not until now, when I look back that I realise just how much I was going to need James over the next few years. Our relationship is known by our friends and family as a whirlwind. We met in the February, I moved in in the April, we got engaged in the May, I fell pregnant in the July and we married in the September. Even now three years on I wouldn't change a thing. Meeting

James was the beginning of my life changing more than I could ever imagine. I finally found the guy that I wanted to spend all my time with, that I wanted to settle down and have children with. I knew that what ever life threw at us, I'd be stronger with him by my side.

Our son was born in the following April and we were enjoying becoming parents. However little did we know that our lives would be turned upside down. I will always remember the night things changed. We had been out for dinner for my stepdad's birthday and my sister Zoe had pulled me to one side on the way into the restaurant.

"Don't panic and don't say anything to anyone tonight, but I just found a lump whilst in the shower before coming out".

My heart jumped a beat, sunk and everything changed in that very second. We snuck off and met in the toilets where Zoe showed me the lump she had found in her breast. At that very moment we both knew. But from that point we also made a pact that we would stay positive, stay calm and take things as they come. After a couple of weeks, appointments, biopsies and scans, Zoe was diagnosed with a fast growing tumour. As a family our lives went on hold and we pulled together to try and be the best support for Zoe as possible. Times were scary and difficult, but we had to have faith in her treatment. My first born was still so small and so I really struggled with juggling a small baby, being a first-time mum and all of a sudden becoming a carer. My sister needed me both during the day and night. Her side effects from the treatment were awful. I was grateful that James was able to take on some of the main care of our son, as Zoe had hospitalisations and treatment every day. I reverted back to how I was when I was a Social Worker. Putting everyone first and not looking after myself. My fibromyalgia was flaring and I was exhausted and in pain. I wasn't able to take the time out to complete my own self care as my sister and baby were my priority. There was no way I was able to return back to Social Work after my maternity leave. My family needed to be my priority. Also the last year had hugely shifted my responsibilities and made me realise I couldn't be and didn't want to be tied to a job.

Being a mum and a carer can really make you lose yourself. You wake up and your day is full of what needs doing for other people. What had previously defined me had gone, I was no longer a well respected professional. That had been all I had known since leaving school. So I was now a thirty year old adult, someone's wife, a mother, a sister that was in a caring role, but what for myself!? I needed to feel like I was achieving something for me as an individual. I needed to challenge my brain again, to help others, but to feel like I was creating revenues for myself. I knew I needed to find something that allowed me to create my own income as that is something I had always been so proud of. I had bought my first house at twenty-four years old on my own and at the age of thirty I owned a four bedroom house. For someone that hadn't been a high flyer at school, or had felt like the bottom of the class, these were my big life achievements so far.

Zoom forward two years on and my sister was free of treatment and free of cancer!! During this time as a family we had been through many ups, and many lows. Cancer has a way of teaching you what is precious in life. Our bodies are so incredible in what they do for us every day. We take for granted how life can change in just one second, in just one passing comment. I now have a little girl who is four months old and my son is two and a half years old. I've become so passionate about helping other people to feel as healthy and as happy as possible. I am still learning so much about what our bodies require to function at their optimal level, but also what we can do to help them and work with them. My health issues had always been things that had held me back or had made life even more difficult. Life can already be so stressful and busy and so self-care needs to be quick, realistic and people need to be able to see and feel results. My journey of chronic ill health has meant I have spent many years on medication. I have experienced so many side effects from drugs that are supposed to have helped me. They are supposed to have enabled me to manage my conditions, but I often felt lost in side effects and never really looked at the triggers of my conditions.

After my daughter was born in lockdown I found myself feeling exhausted, de motivated and losing control of my health again. I knew I needed something that would give me the boost I required. Never did I think it would be the next thing I wanted to share with people. Just one simple coffee a day gave me so many health benefits. I only ever now take or use products that are made from natural ingredients, as I think it's important to look after our bodies and to reduce the toxic load they have to deal with. So when I realised I'd found simple alternatives that gave me so much energy, stopped me napping, gave me motivation, helped me lose weight and enabled me to be a better parent because of all these things, I had to share it with others. I now have so many customers that have had that same hallelujah moment that I had. Alongside this I have been able to turn the property I bought on my own before I was married into a rental income. I have also purchased motorhomes which are now rented out and am currently in the process of buying a holiday let. If the last two years have taught me anything it's that residual income is so important. To be able to work from my phone anywhere is invaluable. I have been able to be there for my sister during her treatment, but also be there as wife and as a mother.

It can be so easy for us to lose ourselves, to lose who we are, what we want in life and what kind of life we want to live. I had been in a job for nine years that I thought was my life, I thought it was the only thing I would ever be good at. In reality life can be so much more than a Monday-Friday job, a nine-to-five job where you're committed to attend in order to earn money. I am forever grateful for all that I learnt during those nine years. I look back with fond memories, even though at times it was tough, dangerous and impacted on my health. It enabled me to create an income as a single person that brought financial freedom. I was able to transfer skills I had learned before into what I am doing now, in that I am still helping people just in a different way. I feel very proud to be able to offer people an alternative they can include in their daily routine that is simple yet effective. So many people are reaching out for quick-fix energy boost that may be filled with empty calories or potentially harmful ingredients. We all live such busy and fast paced lives which can often leave us feeling like we are just existing. So, in order to help people to become the best versions of themselves I support them to find better health and wellbeing through products with natural ingredients.

When I look back on what I have achieved since school I do so with fond memories. Whilst at the time it felt like a battle, trying to juggle ill health and a lack of academic ability; I got through. We all have different definitions and perceptions of achievement. For me now I am happy with where I am. I am present as a parent to my toddler and baby from a health point of view. I am able to juggle my incomes from my phone wherever I may be and should I be needed by a family member I am available. I have dreams of running my own retreat in Scotland, but for now a little holiday let is my first step in that direction. I wake up each day with chronic health issues, but I also wake up each day with ways of managing them and not letting them hold me back.

I always did something I was a little not ready to do. I think that's how you grow. When there's that moment of 'Wow, I'm not really sure I can do this,' and you push through those moments, that's when you have a breakthrough."

———

MARISSA MAYER

Chapter 5

The Journey Back To Myself

Laura Malcolm - Nuttall

Laura is a mindful Mum who is super proud of her three little sunshines. Laura is following her purpose by Training as an Integrative Therapist and Mindset Coach. Sharing her journey through this chapter of the winding road of life to where she is today.

Laura is educated, experienced and entrepreneurial creating a party décor business and owning rental properties. Her philosophy is to be grateful for each moment yet to also be continually growing and challenging herself. She aspires to empower individuals to be their true self and seeks to share knowledge around emotional intelligence and psychology to empower children and adults to gain self-understanding and awareness to improve their wellbeing. Laura dreams of setting up her own wellbeing practice one day in the future… watch this space!

Facebook: Laura Malcolm-Nuttall
Podcast: @abeautifulmind_podcast
Personal: @laura_malcolmnuttall
Professional: @laura_themindsetmentor
www.themindsetacademy.co.uk

Growing up and at school I was really academic and always found learning easy and exciting. I loved studying and always planned on going to university. At school my best subjects were English and business studies, business studies was my favourite as I had a really inspiring teacher and loved to learn all about organisations and people. I believe some of this interest stemmed from living within an entrepreneurial family, my father owned his own building company and mum had started her own second hand clothes agency. There had also been other ventures throughout the years such as a sandwich round, a fruit and vegetable shop amongst other things! I feel this taught me that it's ok to take a risk and give things a go!

During my senior school I didn't have an easy time, I suffered a lot of bullying and the school wasn't the best at pushing children so I came out of school doing very well despite the support on offer and was looking forward to my university experience. I don't ever remember getting any dedicated career guidance at school so made my choice based on my favourite subjects and chose business studies for my degree as I felt it would open up a lot of opportunity. My parents split up during my schooling when I was thirteen which was an upsetting time, but thankfully they remained civil to each other and close to me which meant I always felt secure and loved.

Throughout University I worked waitressing in bars and restaurants which I absolutely loved! Being sociable and being around people was something I truly enjoyed. I undertook my business studies degree at the University of Liverpool and came out with a 2.1. I didn't really know at that point what I wanted to do, so I was offered a job interview by a friend of my Dads where I ended up with my first job. I then steadily progressed within roles in the manufacturing industry such as Personal Assistant to the Director, Office Manager and then onto Business Manager. I was very career driven at this point in life I was in my mid twenties and hadn't really considered having a family anytime soon.

I had met my partner during my university years and we were both very career driven and had bought our first home which was a big renovation project – as dad was a builder I had him on call for support for our project. This was a really exciting time, our new home, a renovation project and great jobs, an active social life full of gigs and festivals with loads of amazing friends! Fun times! At this point in life I was very sure of myself, doing well at work, progressing in my private life and on the property ladder…. Up, up, up. I decided to undertake a Masters Degree in Quantity Surveying in my own time as I believed this was the route I wished to progress into. During this time I was in a great role in a great international company. I was headhunted by another local company and promised the world, I decided to take this opportunity and gave my notice.

The first day on the new job came and as soon as arrived I knew I had made a big mistake, the role was nothing as promised and there definitely was no room for career progression. The feeling I felt that day I will always remember, sitting at the desk with tears welling up in my eyes and a sick feeling in my stomach. I rang my mum on my break and poured my heart out to her about how much I regretted leaving my old role, but I had to get on with it and do the best I could with the situation. This time was a flat time in my career and then the recession hit which meant my dreams of becoming a quantity surveyor were also dashed as the roles on offer were well below my wage expectations so I just couldn't take the jump.

It was at this time my body clock started to kick in as I was in my late twenties. I had not much considered children in my career path at all and it came as a surprise when I started feeling broody. I was blessed to get married to my partner at the age of twenty-nine and my partner's mum had just passed away with cancer which left us with a void which we decided to take the plunge and tried for our first child as it felt like the timing was right and we needed some sunshine in our life. We were engaged and had our wedding booked for 2013, and my first baby, my beautiful son Thomas was born in 2012. Everything changed at that moment, all those career aspirations I had just faded into such a different perspective. I never expected that I would feel the way I did about having children as I had been so career focussed when I was younger it came as a shock to those around me also as they never saw me as very maternal until now!

I still needed to work after maternity but it was a job that fitted with mum life. I left that company I had been so disappointed with and sought out a new role as I needed part time work to fit around my new world and changed priorities. I found an amazing job that taught me a lot about myself and the path I now am pursuing in my career. I began working as an office manager but this was within a charity which provided a care home for people with brain injuries and specialised disabilities.

I built lovely relationships with the residents as I managed their finances and ensured they were as empowered as possible. I loved this job so much and my work felt so much more rewarding than any work I had done before. Sadly the role was made redundant which was very sad but I was so thankful for the experience and relationship I had whilst working there it made me realise that working for a charity could feel so rewarding.

As a new mum I had recently got married and we were planning another baby quite soon, I was on the lookout again for a job that fitted with mum life. These jobs can be difficult to find as there are lots of mums seeking that work life balance. I found it difficult to find a suitable role but did find a remote working role doing twenty hours a week which appeared to offer me a solution. I loved working remotely as I could be around a lot more, get the washing done, clean the house on lunch etc! I stayed with this job whilst having two further children all within a five year period! It was hectic to say the least, during this time we also moved house and undertook on an extension project, crazy as it may sound! During this time I look back now and wonder how I coped at all, living in a house that was non-functional, three small babies to look after, my husband had a health scare during this time too which also brought some dark days.

I was juggling a lot of things and felt so thinly spread that I couldn't do a great job at anything. My work role changed and added more stress to the situation which led me to decide to leave work. One example of the pressure getting too much was when I was attending a trade show for work; I had left very early one morning for the train, leaving my little boys and breastfeeding little girl was emotionally hard, I just felt I didn't want to be at work and my priorities were at home, that pull felt unbearable. I had a panic attack on the train that day, the overwhelming feeling of home sickness and that I was needed much more by my family than by my work, that was probably the moment I made the decision to leave my job.

Back at home my family and husband knew I had been going under, I had been suffering depression, feeling low and overwhelmed, having the panic attack was the final straw. I was still functioning, taking the children out and about, keeping up with tasks but feeling so low on the inside and struggling to get up each day. Leaving work was a relief, taking a step back from career and focusing on the children helped for a little while. I focussed on the children which made me happy and took some breathing space. The house extension took over a year to complete as we project managed it ourselves as that was the only way we could afford the work, this was a big challenge. So as you may imagine this time of our life was chaotic and it makes me a little sad that these are the times when life should be settled so you can truly focus on the new babies arrival. But sometimes timing is a luxury and we cant choose when we make these steps for the bigger picture and the need for a larger house coincided with having the children. We are very thankful now I may add as we have a beautiful big home for the children to enjoy so the painful times have been worth it!

As I took that time out from work I also experienced a lot of guilt as I believe I am a career driven woman I also felt guilt for not pursuing my career goals, you can never win can you?! The compromise of career for being mum hit me hard as all the progression you work for is suddenly spin on it's head as I then prioritised the children over everything. All the hard work I had put in I reflected on and I took some time to have a deep think about my work and was it fulfilling me?

My degree I had achieved at University in business studies had given me a great foundation for every job I ever held and growing up in entrepreneurial family had inspired me to one day have my own business. I had always wanted to try something and now was the time to start thinking about it. My father in law had some money he said he would invest if I had a business idea so I started getting creative. The time and space I had gained from leaving my job gave me some headspace to think about what I really wanted and what career step may be more fulfilling and also fit around the children for the future. I felt very blessed and supported to be able to take this time out, it was only about six months I took off before I initiated my counselling course and also started up my exciting new venture…

I decided to do a few things not just one! I decided to start a party décor business as I had noticed an opportunity in the market, I could start this business up straight away and get trading quite quickly. I also decided to pursue my longer term goal of becoming a qualified counsellor, this course would take three years in total.

Starting up my party décor business was a journey in itself. I had very low self confidence at this time as I had work home so long remotely and I had low self esteem, I had lost Laura somewhere along the way. I was very capable of the business side due to my business degree and managed this all very well. I was very creative also, I made lots of props such as artificial floral numbers, Love letters for weddings, floral backdrops etc. I loved getting creative and lost myself in the moment with my glue gun and flowers for hours! I loved the creativity and really feel running the business fulfilled a part in me that always knew I would be an entrepreneur.

As I mentioned I grew up around entrepreneurship and risk taking and I do like to push myself through my comfort zones. I knew I needed to do this to get my old self back, I used to be so confident and self assured prior to having my children so I believed I could do it.

Once my party décor stock was ready to market I challenged myself and went to networking meetings, wedding shows and offered free setups to local hotels and businesses. I look back at this time and on the inside I felt so small and it felt so scary but the personal growth I felt was massive.

Within a year I could see the difference in my eyes. There is one photo of me taken at the first event I did and I remember that day so clearly feeling so insignificant and unworthy of being there and so shy of a photograph… flash forward to a year later and I took a similar photo at a wedding show and I posed acting silly for the picture and I shocked myself at how far I had come! I would never have done that the year before. So as much as starting my business was for business sake it was for myself and me to prove to myself that I can do it and also gaining the old Laura back.

Currently day-to-day I am very busy but seek to be a mindful mamma, focussing on the precious moments with my little ones but also pushing forward to the bigger goals and vision for the future. I work three days a week as a property consultant, a job I love doing as I love nosing round houses, visualising the potential in properties and meeting a wonderful variety of people of different walks of life. After having worked remotely for so long, getting out the house to work feels so good, I love being part of a team again and the social interaction has meant my confidence has grown and I feel I have my identity again.

My experience in property refurbishment and property investment are valued in this role and I find this job easy and enjoyable to do. This opportunity came about from me taking my own initiative. A long time ago a seed was planted in my mind, when viewing our first home we bought I looked at the lady estate agent and thought... I would like that job, that looks like a cool job. That was around ten years ago!

When I decided to seek a part time role when my daughter turned two I instantly thought of a local estate agent who we had let some of our properties through, I sent an email outlining my background and how I loved the way they worked and would like to be part of their team if they had any opportunities. They created a role just for me! Which was a great confidence boost and I am very grateful for as a mum it can be really difficult to find roles that fit around our priorities as mum. When making the decision to pursue my studies to become a counsellor... during my time of reflection I thought about all the jobs I had done and the time working at the charity stuck out in my mind as feeling very rewarding, also my long term best friend from school had trained as a counsellor which inspired me to this career, I reflected in myself and realised I had a natural ability with people around me, being the person people turned to for support and a listening ear.

I get a gorgeous feeling inside when I am supporting others, I don't call it helping as I like to empower people to use their own power and inner strength that we can often forget we have. I used to think everyone opened up to others in such a way but then I realised it was actually an ability I had and I decided to build on this strength and pursue a career in counselling and coaching. I undertook my level two and three in the summer of 2018 and what a journey it has been since! The self understanding and self development throughout my course has been amazing, after feeling I had lost a lot of my identity through motherhood I now feel much more empowered about who I am. Studying this course has improved my relationships in my own personal life and I believe I can also use my skills to support my children through challenges they may face through life which is also so beneficial. The journey is never ending and I love learning about psychology, therapies and theories.

I have an ever expanding book shelf and have never felt so much on the right path as I do now. I feel I have found my purpose which feels amazing, doing work that really makes a difference is so rewarding. Currently on my level four which is my last year of my three years of study. I am training to be an integrative counsellor which means I can call upon a number of therapies when working with client issues allowing me to support clients with any challenge they may face. I am currently on placement which means working face to face with clients. My journey through my studies has been challenging sharing my precious time between being mum, wife, friend, student and just being me! My vision for the future is to have my own private practice and personal development centre. I dream of empowering people with knowledge, self understanding and self-belief to live a happy and fulfilled life. I feel filled up with joy and fulfilment when supporting others to be their best self.

Quotes I live by:

Cherish the little things
Gratefulness creates a beautiful world
Perspective is everything
We always have a choice
Grow through challenges
Be your own best friend!

Do what you love and success will follow. Passion is the fuel behind a successful career."

MEG WHITMAN

Chapter 6

Rising Like a Phoenix

Georgina Tang

Georgina Tang came to England from Hong Kong at the tender age of thirteen without speaking a word of English and was forced to leave home with £1 in her pocket when she was only sixteen years old. Irrespective of a very difficult start in life and a foreign country, which she now regards as her home country. She achieved several undergraduate and post-graduate degrees in Psychology, Sociology, Housing Management, Strategic Leadership and Management by the time she reached thirty. Not only did Georgina achieved greatly in the academic world, she is also a very successful woman entrepreneur but most important thing to her, mum to Alessio, her lovely caring son with complex educational and medical needs.

She is a known workaholic, managing two businesses and doing freelance work with the Care Quality Commission, as well as being a Governor for a local children's hospital. Therefore, life can be very hectic and stressful, however, she has always managed to spend quality time with her family. She loves going to her holiday home deep in the National Snowdonia Park regularly to de-stress and re-charge her batteries.

Here's the links for her multi award winning business website and social media platforms:

www.ynny.co.uk

Facebook: @YNNY.UK
Instagram: @yoursnaturallynaturallyyours

My journey to success

Yours Naturally Naturally Yours Limited, my skincare business, exists because of the life I've lived – a life characterised by equal measures of challenge and joy - much like the lives of any of you reading this story today. Each of us is on a journey in life, learning from the lessons we embrace, and each of us has the potential to turn the challenging experiences of modern life into positive and tangible outcomes. It simply takes determination, self-belief and a few magic ingredients!

It is the practice of embracing the rough times, and using them to facilitate progress, that has, in part, enabled me to develop the strong ethical and philosophical core values that underpin Yours Naturally Naturally Yours Limited; as managing director of the company, I have always tried to use my experiences and life lessons, to grow a business that offers positive and beneficial solutions to health and skincare challenges. I am proud of what my company has achieved to date, a result of listening to my customers and acting on feedback received. Extensive research has also led to the sourcing of superior natural products that work to complement skin and hair, so we can offer creams, serums and haircare products that really work. But I will never rest on my laurels; I see life, and my business, as part of my ongoing journey, and I will continue to learn, listen and reflect in order that I continue to offer the very best skin care range I can. To make use of an old cliché, when life has thrown me lemons, I've always been determined to find a way to make the very best lemonade I can. And if I can share one of the secrets of my success, it will always be this; life is what you make it. So, grit those teeth, take the positives from difficult situations, and make the decision to flourish; do this, and you WILL make it.

This is my story.

In 1976, when I was thirteen-years-old, my beloved grandma passed away. I was living in Hong Kong with my sisters at the time; we were separated from the rest of the family who had been living in the U.K., throughout the 1970s, running a catering business. My grandma, always a strong-willed character, had died of pneumonia as we had no money to get her seen by a doctor. To lose this beloved figure in my life was a shock, to say the least, and this was my very first experience of heartbreak. Such was my distress, my older sister thought it best to send me to join my family in England where, she reasoned, I would be supported by my parents and brothers. But things were not to prove so simple.

My parents had a Chinese Takeaway business and it was barely surviving. As a result, we ate the food leftovers that we couldn't sell to customers. Indeed, our takeaway took so little money that our accountant did our books for free for years, as we simply had nothing with which to pay him. I had made the journey from one country to another, suffered a bereavement, and was now witnessing my family struggling – enough of a challenge to any teenager. However, I knew what my grandmother would have wanted me to do; she would have told me to roll up my sleeves and get stuck in – which is exactly what I did, teaching me that hard work and dedication are what sees you through adversity. I also realised that, whilst some of my school friends didn't receive a hot meal each day, at least I did. This positive outlook, nurtured by familiar experiences, is definitely a life-lesson I have carried throughout my time on this planet…and to think it all started behind the counter of a Chinese takeaway!

Naturally, life as a Chinese immigrant was not always easy, especially when cultural challenges and nuances were thrown into the mix for good measure. My mother was what one might call a 'difficult woman', and I had had little contact with her before moving to England. This caused tensions between us living under one roof. In addition, when I look back – isn't hindsight a wonderful thing? - I realise she also had to contend with something unimaginable, something that explains her seeming inability to show maternal tenderness. She had other things on her mind; the very real fact was, she lived daily in the knowledge that my father was in love with another woman.

He had married out of duty to his family; arranged marriages were an accepted part of our culture and he was bound early on in his life to marry a woman, or rather the child bride, that my mother was. She had been purchased at eight-years-old, the result of her brother's gambling addiction; the sale of my mother paid her brother's debts and my mother was then bound, by law, to marry my father when he reached twenty-one. My childhood was, as a result, challenging to say the least. In modern parlance, one could say I suffered psychological and physical abuse, only enjoying respite when my grandmother had intervened, taking me away from my mother – a woman deeply disturbed in her own way. This is another reason I felt the loss of my grandmother so viscerally. That I survived that time, is a miracle, but survive I did – an instinct that has driven me forward in life and in business to this very day.

In life, I always think there's balance. And for every negative, there's a positive. My positive took the form of a careers officer, David Akerman. He counselled me through the school leaving process in my sixteenth year. A kindly and sensitive soul, he picked up on some of the challenges I was encountering with my family, and he supported me in securing my first paid position as a mother's help with a Jewish family. Accommodation came as part of the deal - which was a bonus. The second bonus was that David became a life-long friend. I left my family home with big dreams and one English pound in my back pocket.

I won't lie; the job was tough. Remember, I was only sixteen years old, a young teenager who should have been enjoying her life; instead I was cooking, cleaning and looking after two children. The job was physically and emotionally demanding but the positive was I had a roof over my head, food to eat, and a small salary which enabled me to taste my first mouthful of independence. It is no accident that I now possess resilience, patience and determination, in everything I endeavour to achieve. My ability to see the good in every situation I am faced with is something that really did start in that first job.

W. B. Yeats once said: Be not inhospitable to strangers, lest they be angels in disguise and David, my careers officer, was that angel. On my day off, I would visit David and his family, who treated me as though I belonged. They showed me what love was, and the importance of having a support network. They were a truly inspirational unit, and definitely the reason I aspire to be the best mother to my wonderful son, Alessio. Many professionals suggest that people from broken homes, and those who have experienced challenging, painful childhoods, enter into a pattern of learned behaviour, repeating the mistakes of the past. I would say, it is the opposite in my case. I am a protective lioness to my darling boy and offer him the upbringing I craved - at any cost – another lesson I picked up on my journey.

I couldn't be a mother's help forever, however. So, after completing my time in that role, I went into nursing - a way of thanking my grandma for looking after me, I suppose. I enjoyed caring for others but I still craved something else, and that 'something missing' was academic learning. As a result, despite people telling me I should just stick at what I was doing, I decided to secure an education, something that had been impossible previously, given the upheaval of my childhood. I decided to study for A-Levels in Psychology and Sociology, alongside washing dishes in a pizza restaurant in Wimbledon. I'm particularly proud of the fact that, whilst I was studying and working, the manager noticed the potential in me to do even better, and promoted me to a waitressing position. This enabled me to expand my curriculum vitae, prove to myself that I could do anything I set my mind to, and, not to be sniffed at, earn more money!

My hard work paid off and I got the grades I needed to study a combined degree in Psychology and Sociology in Liverpool. The only problem was that my father refused to sign my grant application because he thought I was a communist – why else would I be studying Sociology? Fortunately, our accountant realised I was not part of The Revolution and agreed to sign the form to enable me to access the education grant. I worked part time throughout my time in university for survival and was lucky to get a job immediately after graduation - working on a new project at the Chinese Community Centre as their first ever health interpreter. Again, I feel that by showing diligence, determination and unwavering commitment, I was setting the foundations for future success in business.

A few years later, I left community work for a trainee housing management job, as it provided a structured career route. Within five years, I obtained a post-graduate foundation and then a post-graduate diploma in Housing Management from Salford University. Furthermore, I obtained a MSc module in Leadership Management from Leeds University. Most important of all, I became Head of Housing with the deputising role for the Chief Executive. I was Chief Executive in waiting and would have been the youngest chief officer in social housing, not to mention the first female from the black and minority ethnic community in such a role. Why should race, gender or age be a barrier to success? It wasn't going to be for me, as where others might see obstacles, I grab opportunities.

Never one to rest, my next challenge was pregnancy. My nine month journey was not what one might call 'plain-sailing'. I suffered life-threatening issues whilst carrying Alessio and, as if that wasn't bad enough, I then realised another challenge was looming. Despite the difficult period I was experiencing, my employer chose that very time to terminate my employment. I might have been sick but, as you've probably guessed by now, I was not going to take this lying down, metaphorically speaking! Literally, I was lying down, of course, but he was not going to get away with such discrimination – pregnancy is no grounds for dismissal! Not one to walk away from difficulties in my life, and with the help with my union GMB, I challenged the arbitrary employer decision. And I won. As I had suspected, my employer was guilty of Sex Discrimination, and I now won the Employment Tribunal, proving that fact.

All of this happened to a rather alarming soundtrack, as it were; I was fighting for justice while experiencing the fear of a traumatic birth – blood loss from me. Breathing cessation from Alessio (he always keeps me on my toes!) And then, I lost consciousness. Probably the best solution given the circumstances! However, what I will say is that I never take a day for granted with my son. I will be forever grateful to the nurses and doctors who saved two lives in one day. And from that experience, I realised that I can do anything. If I ever doubt myself, I tap in to my positivity reserves because I, more than most, know that anything is possible.

Birth was just the beginning though. Let me clarify! I realise that birth is a beginning for everybody, but Alessio's birth was only the start to what has been a terrifying, beautiful, frustrating, exhilarating wonderful, unforgettable, frightening, but always wonderful, section to my story. I closely and obsessively nursed Alessio during the first three years of his life because he had a tendency to stop breathing without any warning, especially when asleep - just to keep me alert! And this taught me another new skill – the ability to function on two hours of sleep. Don't underestimate this string to your bow when starting out in business!

As if that wasn't enough for my warrior son to contend with, Alessio was also diagnosed as having complex medical and educational needs when he was four-years-old. He is autistic and will require life-long support but we take each day in our stride, my beautiful son is now seventeen-years-old, and enjoys life to the fullest, not bad for a boy who was predicted by a consultant not to reach his first birthday. He is my miracle and he makes me believe in the impossible every day of my life!

That's not to say there wasn't some learning opportunities along the way. When Alessio had to undergo chemotherapy for his Juvenile Idiopathic Arthritis, I noticed very early on that he was developing skin problems, as many undergoing chemo tend to do. In addition, around the same time, my neighbour was suffering the after effects of breast cancer treatment – hair loss and skin hypersensitivity. And, of course, these problems needed a solution - which leads me to December 2011. I decided to attend a free bath bomb and soap making course offered by FACE in Liverpool – a decision that proved to be life-changing. After attending some more courses, I began making natural skin care products as, both a hobby, and a means of developing something that could potentially help my neighbour and my son.

The birth of my company, Yours Naturally Naturally Yours Limited, was a direct result of wanting to help alleviate the suffering of two people I hold very dear. It then became an obsession to offer quality products that could help anybody, anywhere – always with the proviso that I would be offering 'skin kind' products. If skin and hair is happy, then I'm happy!

My hobby - making products on the kitchen table, just like the inspirational late Anita Roddick of Body Shop – has led me to where I am today. Yours Naturally Naturally Yours Limited employs several local people, and all our products are handmade in our headquarters in Widnes, Cheshire. Our range includes ultra-mild shampoos and conditioners, skin creams, body butters, serums, soy candles, massage oils and anything and everything in between. If there's a need, then I will seek to develop a product to meet that need, my motivation always being my son. If he can laugh and smile through his autism, severe health and learning difficulties, then anything is possible. He is my inspiration, my joy, my life.

I am proud of how far the company has developed. My clients come from the beauty industry across UK and the globe, and the company is always expanding as more people recognise and accept that natural and organic products are far preferable and more effective than those laced with chemicals. I love creating and making skin and haircare products that make people feel good about themselves, and that's why I am so passionate about creating high quality products at affordable prices.

From having one pound in my pocket forty-one years ago, and nowhere to live, I now have a successful business and a portfolio of properties. And that's not all. I do freelance inspection work with the Care Quality Commission and have been a long standing Governor for Alder Hey Hospital, (second home for Alessio) as I am passionate about children's health care. I am a workaholic but I still find time to go away to our holiday home in North Wales regularly to have some quality family time to de-stress – and to think about my next product, of course!

My life experiences have enabled me to become a firm believer in miracles. They do happen. And I aim to share the magic in whatever small way I can – which is basically a shameless plug for our Elixir Serum; it is a magical potion – a miracle in a bottle, if you like. If I could bottle my life experiences, this is what it would look and smell like!

If I could share one last lesson with you, it would be this: Don't let fear stop you from achieving your dreams, because dreams do come true. Dare to believe.

And in the words of one YNNY customer: Don't stop making these small miracles …. we need you.

And, isn't happy customer feedback the highest praise of all.

There is nothing like a concrete life plan to weigh you down. Because if you always have one eye on some future goal, you stop paying attention to the job at hand, miss opportunities that might arise, and stay fixedly on one path, even when a better, newer course might have opened up."

INDRA NOOYI

Chapter 7

Big shoes to fill, My Way

Francesca Manca

Fran is a mum, an entrepreneur, a jazz singer, a pinup, and a viking re-enactor. And of course, a crazy cat lady. She is Italian but Liverpool and its wonderful people adopted her in 2010 and never let her go.

She fights for what she thinks is right, campaigns for PDA awareness and she never shies away from the truth.
She love weightlifting, skiing, and has a deep love with hot yoga.
You can find her anywhere where good food is served, behind a pile of books or on long beaches.

She is the founder of Underwing where she helps female founders and special needs entrepreneurs turn their ideas into fully formed businesses.

www.underwingliverpool.com

Instagram: @underwinglpl
Facebook: @underwinglpl
Twitter: @underwinglpl

My name is Francesca Giuditta Eleonora Manca and I am the founder of Underwing, where I help female founders being seen by setting themselves apart from the competition, and special needs entrepreneurs creating successful, fulfilling careers with no meltdowns, sensory overload, or need for masking.

Named after my grandma (nonna) and my great-grandmother, I have always been proud of my long, weird name, which comes with big shoes to fill, the shoes of two amazing women; one who did what she really wanted, when this was not the fashion - my great grandmother Maria Angelica Eleonora left her arranged marriage to be with the love of her life at the beginning of the 20th century - and the other one who used her life to change the world for the better as much as she could - my grandmother Francesca built schools in Africa since the 1980s and devoted her whole life to helping others.

It's a weird family, mine, full of both dynasties of 'traditional' jobs - my father is a lawyer, like his grandfather, his uncle, his great-grandfather, and so on and people who went to extreme lengths to realise their dream, their calling in life my grandfather Mauro Manca was forced to get a 'proper job' with the city council in order to marry Nonna Francesca, job which he quit soon after the wedding to follow his dream of being a painter, becoming one of the most prominent figures of the Italian Futurism and Material Painting.

My maternal grandmother Nonna Terina rescued herself and her seven siblings from Tunisia during the second world war working as a seamstress, and then she met my grandfather nonno Pino who, to guarantee she would never have to work another day in her life, went from selling gas bottles to owning and running the biggest furniture store in Sardinia, Italy, where I come from.

So this is the environment I grew up in. A family full of examples of the fact that 'having a university degree and a safe job is the road to success', but also, on the other hand, of incredible stories of willpower, dedication, and success to fulfilling your purpose in life against all odds.

I had a happy, uneventful, really lucky and comfortable childhood, I lived in Sardinia, where the sea, the sun and dream-like beaches made days slow and easy for about four months a year. Where a group of those who are still my lifelong friends were there to support and challenge me, together with my many (about thirtyish) cousins, and the female figures who have inspired me for the forty-three years I have been on this earth: my grandmothers, my mum Giacomina, my aunties, my two sisters Caterina and Elena, and my best friends Angela, Piera, Pina, Monica.

These women have been there always, they are examples of strength, courage, kindness, fierceness, intelligence, elegance, determination, compassion.
They have supported me, loved me, pushed me, they stood up to me when it was needed, told me off. They have celebrated and grieved with me, and I would not be where I am now without their support. And then there's my dad. The first love of my life. The man I grew up trying to please, who has put up with all of my nerdiness (is this a word?), weirdness, with being so different from my mates, with my strong head and my tendency to do everything my way, never stopping me, always supporting me, even when he really didn't approve.

These people have helped shape my life into what it is now, and even today, while we live hundreds of miles apart, they are a big part of my support net.

Sardinia is an amazing place to grow up in, but also one I wanted to run away from. So after my happy, sunny childhood and classical studies in high school, I decided to go to university and do Psychology in Rome. Truth is, I had no idea in heaven of what I wanted to do in my life, I just wanted to 'help people' and go to Rome, live by myself, feel 'grown up', sing, and generally get away from a place the mentality of which was too restrictive and restricted, for my liking.

University life was amazing, light and free. After it, I moved to Milan, and this is where my life seriously changed for the first time. My sister and I took jobs as Fieramilano Stewardesses and tour leaders. I was a natural at that, I loved making the event run smoothly and managing people. I started working for the agencies organising the events, and in the blink of an eye I was being promoted, planning and running events for four thousand people for the likes of DIESEL and Santander. I LOVED IT. I was made for it. I adored every single step from planning, to production, and post-event budget tally-up.

My career in events lasted for some successful years, in which I lived in Milan and travelled to and from Liverpool, where my best friend was doing a PHD in history, and where I met my ex husband. With him I lived in Milano, where my son was born in 2009, for a couple of years, before moving back to Liverpool, which has since become my happy home. I ADORE Liverpool. The people, the history, the beaches, the forests, the vibrant life, the huge variety of live shows/theatres/ concerts. I am a fierce advocate of this city and I consider myself an adopted Scouser.

In Liverpool, my life and career changed once more, in many ways.
In 2015, when my son was six, after a lifetime of difficulties in preschool first and school after, he was permanently excluded from mainstream school. This triggered a moment of research for us parents which culminated into a diagnosis of PDA

(pathological demand avoidance, a part of the autism spectrum) and an eighteen months tribunal battle against the local authority, so that my son could get the education he was entitled to. It also started a huge learning curve for me, so that I could understand PDA better and help people do the same. Because of the lack of information about PDA in italian, I started the first blog, fb group and youtube channel to raise awareness, share techniques, etc., and in the last five years I have been helping families and schools understand PDA and work better with their children/ pupils. (www.autismopdaitalia.com / youtube Francesca Manca 'Techniche PDA in 10 minuti')

In 2016, my ex husband and I divorced and I became a single mum. The battle against LEA was won and my son entered an AMAZING school in which he is understood, helped and valued for his abilities, instead of being penalised for the limits PDA imposes on him.

My job also changed, I moved from purely events, to events and marketing, then marketing and business consultancy, working in big agencies first, B2B after, till one day, at the very beginning of 2018, I was made redundant and took the plunge, becoming a self-employed marketing and business consultant with the trading name of FMSquared Marketing.
My clients were varied and needed the most diverse services, from social media to branding and business strategy. Business grew and it was difficult for me to stay on top of work and still help PDA families.
Also, the more I got to know parents of children like my son, and talk to them, the more it was clear to me that a range of professional services aimed at people with special needs was sorely needed in Italy and UK. And then one day, during a hot yoga lesson, it hit me. This was MY JOB, this was MY OPPORTUNITY, MY CALLING.

My job in this life is to channel all the amazing nonne and nonni I had, and set aside from the flocks by doing something no one had done before, which would make the world a better place and guarantee that people like my son would have somewhere to turn to when entering their career and adult lives.

And so, despite everyone warning me that I was narrowing my field too much, and I wouldn't find enough clients, my rebranding was born. With the help of the amazing Matchstick Agency in Liverpool I created a new branding, aimed at female founders and special needs entrepreneurs.
Underwing is a safe space where all my clients are kept 'under my wing' while they learn how to fly solo.

Underwing is a place where we work together to help your idea become a business, so you can soar like never before.

No matter your circumstances, the limits imposed by having to care for your children while running a business, or by your special needs, we use our business and marketing knowledge to create a plan of action and help your career fly, taking into consideration your circumstances and resources.

I am pleased to report that 'everyone' was wrong, and Underwing is indeed a very successful business!

In 2019 I started seeing a pattern in what my one-two-one clients with special needs were telling me: "it's great to work with you and have this knowledge and these tools now, if only school or university, had prepared them for what working life would have been" …

And so a new program was born.

The Underwing's "Shaping your Future" program brings into schools, colleges and universities a series of workshops for special needs students, aimed at helping these individuals to identify their passions, skills, and take into consideration their needs when choosing a job/career; write a business plan if they have a business idea; create and market their business and overcome their unique needs.

This project, now I know, is the fulfilment of my career, as it puts together my skills and knowledge while solving a problem which affects so many, including my son.

Helping women and special needs entrepreneurs realising their dreams and creating successful and fulfilling careers is so much more than I thought I could do when I set off to do psychology because 'I wanted to help people'. My journey as a special needs mum, everything that happened in my life and my amazing support network are what led to this. And the reason why I tell my story is that, along my path, I work with so many amazing parents, especially mums, who have so many entrepreneurial ideas about services or products which could really impact the lives of children like ours, but never find the confidence to even get the ball rolling.

To these women I want to say, I am you. And you are me. You CAN create a business that puts your skills and the knowledge of your children's special needs together, and makes the world a better place for them.

No matter what other people say, no matter the circumstances, your drive comes from the deepest love known to mankind, and I can assure you you WILL succeed. Just make a plan, and take the first step. You've got this.

"At the end of the day, you are the only one that is limiting your ability to dream, or to actually execute on your dreams. Don't let yourself get in the way of that."

———

FALON FATEMI

Chapter 8

100% Unemployable

Danielle Hobson

Danielle Hobson is the founder of the Build a Business Academy and The Mum Does Business Membership!

She coaches women who are looking to have it all in life, business success and present parenthood through helping them realise their true potential, building their dreams and being truly successful in their own right.

www.daniellehobson.co.uk

Facebook: @DHCoaching

Facebook Group: Mumpreneurs Society

I started life in the South Yorkshire town of Doncaster. I'm still very much a northern girl born and bred. Still living in Doncaster surrounded by my friends and family.

My childhood was what I would call a 'normal' working-class childhood. My parents were and still are together and happily married. My mum was a stay at home mum and my dad worked any job he could to pay the bills. We didn't have an extremely wealthy life but it suited my parents and we traveled once a year to Spain from the age of seven. I am the oldest of three siblings and at times felt like the third parent. I felt like I grew up quicker than I perhaps needed to but I think this was a lot to do with the fact I am Miss Independent and extremely ambitious, always wanting to know more, do more, and have more.

I left home at seventeen, quit college at eighteen, and fell pregnant at nineteen!
I suffered from domestic violence for four and a half years from my son's dad.
THIS DOES NOT DEFINE ME!
But what it did do even though I didn't know it until later was play a big part in who I am today. Which is why I still mention it.
I learned so much from that relationship that I carried it through my life to this day.
One of the lessons was how NOT to raise my son.

Dropping out of college three-quarters of the way through the course looking back was probably one of the most valuable lessons in my life. I regretted it so much that it gave me one of my biggest traits, Tenacity! Some people will say stubborn, I say tenacious.
If I truly believe in something, I am with it till death.

Soon after I left college I fell into a job in health and social care, working in a local care home, I believed it was all I was good for. I started at £3.75 per hour. What actually happened was I loved it, I felt like my young life had a purpose. All those beautiful souls who had served all of their lives were now depending on little old me. I made them smile, laugh, and cared for them in a way that lit me up. This gave me my first idea of what I could do in the future. I wanted my very own care agency. And I had always had the goal of owning my own business at some point, I hated taking instructions. I could see how doing what I loved and becoming self-employed would be perfect for me.

But at the tender age of nineteen, I found out I was pregnant with my son Mason! Lots of emotions because of the relationship I was in but I was adamant about making it work and not giving up. I was so wrong, what actually happened was we split up badly when Mason was two weeks old.

Single Mum........Was not in my life's plan.

I had a mortgage, a house to keep, a baby, and a full-time carers job and I had just turned twenty years old. I felt my only option was to go back to work full time when my son was four months old so I could keep the roof over our heads. I didn't ask for help and wouldn't, couldn't, shouldn't, right?!
This was me being stubborn.

Time flew by, I moved through companies within the health and social care sector, looking for the best opportunities to progress and up my knowledge, experience, and skills in the industry.

I met my now-husband when Mason was nearly one, whirlwind romance.
As I write this we have been together for thirteen years and life has been crazy good since we met. We have had another baby, Lilly, now nine.

When I had Lilly, it all came crashing down around me, I suffered from postnatal depression, I couldn't be away from Lilly, I had huge guilt from the time I had Mason at the fact that I didn't spend enough time with him when he was a baby and that then came flooding back when I had Lilly. I spent the next couple of years after a year's maternity trying to find a better opportunity to tick all boxes, allowing me to spend more time with the kids but also feed the hunger I had to be successful.

I was twenty-seven and nowhere near the care agency I had planned on having by then.

I needed to find something else.

It was like fate, the year I decided something needed to change was the year I stumbled on a business opportunity to work from home. 2014 I started on the road of network marketing. I had no knowledge of the products, company, or industry but it sounded amazing, I was sold.

I had found a new calling. It was still helping people with their health and wellbeing just with products instead of personal care.

Within six months of working the business very part-time around a full-time job, a three-year-old, and a seven-year-old, I had overridden my wage four times over.
It was a no brainer, that was when I quit the j-o-b!
24th July 2015 was the last day I ever worked for someone else.

My word! I was ecstatic. Had I really made it into the self-employed world? Had I really got my very own business? Was I really earning all this money?
YES! YES! YES! Was the answer.

What I really loved the most about what I did then was that I could help other women like myself do exactly what I had done. I was present in my kid's lives, not working silly shifts. And I was also successful as DANIELLE, doing what I loved. Because I dare say this now without feeling the guilt but...I wasn't just put on this earth to be a mum.

I spent my days coaching and mentoring women all over the world to do more, have more, and be more.

This continued for five years under the umbrella of the network marketing company I had joined in 2014. But in 2019 I had this huge urge to go solo, concentrating on just the coaching side of the business, helping mums start their own businesses from scratch under the name of Danielle Hobson Coaching.

I retrained in business, life, and mindfulness coaching, I am an NLP and EFT practitioner also. I worked on my own mindset so much over the five years I had been in business, it felt only right that I also share that with other women too.

That was it - I had actually found my calling! It had never felt so right. I attracted clients straight away and I was on a roll.

So now I still help mums start their own businesses as well as getting a hang of their mindsets tackling those limiting beliefs that hold us back from doing what we really should and could be doing. I work from home, around my husband and children.

I have three ways in which you can work with me......

My membership program club (MDB Club) offering everything you need in online training workshops and coaching sessions.

My signature twelve-week program delivered one to one and tailored to each client, helping them start and grow their business.

Eight-week group coaching program - based on business basics from mindset and idea defining to gaining clients/customers.

If I could give you any advice in life it would be to never hold back, follow your actual calling/passion. Do what actually lights you up until it doesn't, then do something else. And always live life like something wonderful and amazing is about to happen, then get ready.

"I've never thought of myself as a female engineer, or founder, or a woman in tech. I just think of myself as someone who's passionate."

LEAH BUSQUE

Chapter 9

Life is a stage!

Andrea Binks

Andrea trained as a dancer and worked extensively around the world as a performer before joining Bid TV. After many years working as a shopping channel presenter and having two children she is is now studying for a BA Hons in Integrative Counselling. Andrea also runs her own health and wellness business, theatre school and enjoys her time as a single mum to her two boys.

After successfully navigating an acrimonious divorce Andrea now uses her knowledge and experience to help other women find happiness again following divorce. Her passion is to inspire others to thrive in their new life.

Facebook: @AndreaBinksBinksy
Instagram: @abbinksy

I always wanted to be a dancer, or a performer. As a little girl I would perform for people and make them laugh. Making people laugh fulfilled a need in me. I now know through my counselling training that that need in me is to be liked but back then I just knew I liked the feeling of people watching me, knowing they were finding what I was doing funny. I had an older sister, Danii, who I absolutely idolised. You would always find me digging around in the bottom of her wardrobe for clothes. Something she hated but she always had better clothes than me, she still does. I just can't fit into her clothes anymore.

As a young child I always had so much energy. That's how I ended up dancing at the age of three. My mum had taken my sister along to help build up her confidence and one day my dance teacher said to my mum 'why don't you leave the baby too' And that was it. My love for dance was born. This was at 'The Georgette Juveniles' Dance School on Canvey Island where I was raised. Georgettes as we called it, was owned and run by a lady called Queenie and boy did Queenie know how to produce some fabulous shows.

I remember performing at the local theatre and absolutely loving every minute. We would perform in dance shows and pantomimes, compete in dance competitions and we even performed Peter Pan where the main cast members got to fly on wires- gosh I was so jealous. I have desperately wanted to recreate these types of shows with my own Theatre School, but times have changed and due to the costs and the risk element involved it's not been possible, yet!

At this point dancing was a firm favourite of mine but I had no idea that it could be a career until my favourite dance teacher 'Linda Selleck' told my mum that I should think about joining a more prestigious school like Italia Conti in London as she believed I had talent and could make it in this exciting but tough profession. WOW I was so excited that my dance teacher had said that I was talented.

I wish I had had the courage to move to a London school at a younger age, but I didn't want to leave the school I was currently at, now called 'Pinkies'. I liked the friends that I had, and truth be told I loved the fact that I got to dance with all the older girls. Big fish little pond as the saying goes. I did however get accepted into dance college when I was fifteen which I absolutely loved.

Never to dream small though, I remember during my audition for Performers the directors asked me what my ultimate job would be following my three years there. I responded that I wanted to direct Hollywood movies. Ha! They told me that they thought perhaps Performers College wasn't quite the right college for me, but I ensured them that 'no it was fine'. I had it all worked out. I confidently told them 'I would train to be a dancer- because I loved it and then after a few years I would become an actress, move to Hollywood and eventually become a director of Hollywood movies!'

Oh, the naivety of a sixteen-year-old air head right. Or was it? OK so Hollywood hasn't happened …yet but I have been directing Theatre shows for the past couple of years. So, it wasn't total nonsense.

I loved my three years at Performers college. I made some lifelong friends and got to dance literally every day, all day. I started dancing professionally during my third year when I was chosen to perform in a John Spillers Panto and then left College with a summer contract dancing for Kim Gavin in the Lily Savage Show in Blackpool. I loved working as a dancer, from cruise ships, to one-nighter's to pantomimes and musical theatre it was so much fun. BUT I still had a dream and I started to want more. This was when I moved into playing some main characters in theatre shows rather than just dancing. My absolute favourite was when I played Wendy in Peter Pan and got to spend all Christmas wearing a nightie, singing and flying around for fun- and being paid to do it It was a dream come true.

I spent many years dancing and singing my way around the world and then one day I saw an advert for 'Bid TV' in The Stage Newspaper. My dream to go bigger kicked in again and I applied. I was so excited when I got offered a screen test and then following that a place as a freelance presenter. I couldn't quite believe it. I remember the excitement and nervousness that I felt during my first day and first full week of training. I found to my surprise that I was quite good at this 'shopping telly' lark. We were trained in talking to camera, researching products and also how to sell just about anything at the drop of a hat.

I remember one of our last exercises during training was when we had spent about twenty minutes prepping a product. I was all set and ready to go to present it and was told at the last second that I wouldn't be selling the item I had researched but a Tesco carrier bag instead! GULP! It just showed though what fantastic trainers I had had as I didn't falter but sold that plastic bag as though my life depended on it.

That was it. I had passed and the next step was going live. My first product was a set of saucepans. I can still remember the outfit I wore and the static speaking I did. Luckily it seemed to go well, and I was off. My sales were good, and I was loving it. When a job on the management team came up, I jumped at the chance to apply.

I was due to get married later that year and we knew we wanted to start a family soon after so going for the staff position felt right at this time. Up until this point I had always worked as a self-employed performer. This was a new life stage for me. I felt anxious to give up the freedom of being self-employed but also an excitement for a bit of security. I got the job! I couldn't believe it.

My new job title was 'Senior Presenter' for 'Sit-up TV' and I would be part of the management team not only presenting three hour shows live on-air but also helping to train any new presenters joining the team. I stayed in this role for eight years moving to part time after my first child was born. I felt weirdly secure but also a bit trapped.

As a freelancer you never really worried too much about booking personal things into your diary and when I agreed to the role my honeymoon was just a few months away. This was a bit of an issue as suddenly I had a 'holiday quota' and I needed more days than I was technically allowed. The company allowed me to work six-day weeks for three weeks to ensure I completed my hours; I was exhausted and not used to these kinds of limitations. But It was all worth it when I was lying on my sunbed in St Lucia drinking cocktails and knowing I was still getting paid- which as a self-employed person you don't get. If you don't work, you don't get paid- it's as simple as that.

During my time working for Sit-up TV. I would still get the odd one nighter dancing gig and also had a couple of other freelance presenting jobs that I could pop in and out of, it was great. Financially though I still wanted more. That's when I found Arbonne, which is a health and wellness company with over forty years in operation.

I instantly fell in love with their products and the idea that you could earn additional income whilst recommending their products. This is perfect I thought, I am naturally recommending things to other people and I love the products so surely this would be an easy add on? Simple! Well not quite so simple. Running an Arbonne business does take a lot of hard work, effort and a great deal of personal development which I wasn't used to at all prior to finding Arbonne.

Personal development, what exactly is it? Well in my opinion it is reading books that enhance your well-being, both mentally and physically. It is enhancing your knowledge, so you are better able to deal with life's ups and downs and boy did I have one huge 'down' coming my way in the form of an extremely acrimonious divorce- that's another story all together and one that I will soon be releasing in my book 'Divorce Daze'.

Fast forward to 2018 and I had moved on from Bid TV and was now hosting for TJC. I started my journey with TJC in 2014, just at the very start of my divorce and then ended it in 2019. You could say I was only there to get me through that devastating time in my life. I am however far happier in my life currently than I was during my five years at TJC. I was never one of the 'favoured' presenters which meant I got given the graveyard shifts. I had to either get up at 3am to get to the studios at 4.30am or I was getting home around 3.30am from the nightshift and there was absolutely zero consistency meaning I was indefinitely tired. My eyes stung continuously, and I found myself just running on empty.

During those five years I had to find something else as I felt the irregular hours were slowly killing me, so I decided to join a Franchise for a Theatre School. I had previously run my own theatre school before I had children, so I had experience in this area and joined a franchise as I no longer wanted to go it alone. So, I bought into New Youth Theatre and ran 'New Youth Theatre Essex' from 2018 until 2020 when the pandemic kicked in. I opted to leave the Franchise during the pandemic purely because It was not fulfilling my need financially.

I am in the process of branding my own Performing Arts school, but this will be performing arts classes with a difference. I will be incorporating mindfulness and meditations into the classes. My new company is called CC Productions and I am excited for what this might bring for me in the future.

As you know by now, I am not one for shying away so I decided to apply for a degree. I got accepted and am currently studying for a degree in Integrative Counselling. I chose this area of study as my divorce caused me so much upset, not only for myself but for my children too. I wanted to be able to help other people navigating these difficult times. I really didn't want anyone else to suffer like I had so I enrolled onto an access course in counselling in 2018- literally at the same time as I opened my New Youth Theatre Essex franchise. I am now just about to go into my Level 5 BA Hons in Integrative Counselling. I am excited and nervous all at the same time which seems to have been a common theme for me with everything I have ever done.

Have you had other jobs?

I class myself as a grafter. From the minute I could get a job I did. My very first job was for BHS in the kitchen department. It was in Lakeside shopping centre and I really enjoyed it. The highlight for me was when someone tried to pay for their goods with a stolen card. As I was trying to process the payment the person just legged it out of the store. The security guard chased after them and brought them to justice but that kept us talking for a good few weeks. To my children's surprise I have also worked for McDonald's. I began by cooking the burgers (apparently every newbie starts on the grills) and I am a vegetarian, so this was hard to do but like I say I am a grafter. Then I was moved onto the tills, most girls were. How sexist looking back now. I remember I was asked to go to the office one day and told that I had been mystery shopped for the famous McDonald's stars! And can you believe it, I failed! Apparently, the burger was the wrong one and the fries were cold. BUT the manager still gave me my stars! I couldn't believe it. I found the whole experience really quite funny. How can I have failed, which I was told 'no one ever fails on their first two stars' and then receive them anyway!

This just goes to show you that even if you can't pass your two-star badge for MacDonald's you can still become a success! I also hated school. I can't actually recall why I hated school so much but I remember saying I hated school a lot. I went to the

Cornelius Vermuyden school on Canvey Island and was in Mabut 1. My tutor group for my year consisted of three boys David, Stuart and Trevor, Me and Medellis who quickly became one of my best friends at Cornelius. I really did quite well at school although my well was never good enough for me.

I was deputy head girl, joint with Medellis naturally but I wanted to be Head girl. I was in the netball team playing wing attack but never the captain. I got five grade A's in my G.C.S.E but I wanted them all to be grade A's. Why I felt like this I don't know but I do believe that passion for more is what has kept me going throughout my life and especially throughout my divorce.

Sadly, my beloved Medellis passed away suddenly in the summer of 2019 and it made me realise that we never really know when our life will come to an end so we need to make sure we do everything we can to enjoy the precious time we do have. I believe that happiness is the ultimate goal in life and I invite you to download my FREE E-book from www.binksy.co.uk on 'how to live a beautiful life'

Thank you for reading my story,

Much love Binksy

We need to accept that we won't always make the right decisions, that we'll screw up royally sometimes – understanding that failure is not the opposite of success, it's part of success."

ARIANNA HUFFINGTON

Chapter 10

Glitter is Life!

Sophie Jones

Sophie spends festival season adding a bit of sparkle and face painting magic to the crowds. She also tailor makes art workshops for all ages, working to a chosen objective or supplied subject.

Her workshops are created and ran in a holistic manner and Sophie would like to develop this side of the business to eventually be her full time job.

Facebook: @gingerislandartsandcrafts
Instagram: @gingerislandartsandcrafts

Art was always my favourite subject at school, and growing up I'd always be making something or sketching away. I was encouraged to do 'Proper A-levels' in the words of my mother, probably having aspirations of me becoming a Brain Surgeon or Pilot like all mothers do. Unfortunately not studying Art did not float my boat, and after two years of scraping through my A-levels, I went back to my beloved Art.

Before I knew it I'd completed my HND in Graphic Design and My BA Hons in Multi-Media Design. Whilst studying I worked on many play schemes in Liverpool and worked on a camp in America delivering art sessions. It was there in America I realised my true vocation was to work with young people. The next step was then to combine my two passions.

I studied for and passed my Post Graduate Certificate in Education specialism Art has which has since allowed me to teach in primary schools and other child settings. Anyone who has competed a P.G.C.E will agree it's possibly one of the most intense years you can go through. Late night calls to my father throwing tantrums like an eight year old were a regular thing. His calming voice and regular words of wisdom were a great support and after twelve months I qualified as a Primary School Teacher. Training and then working in such roles I realised that there was a market to use my specialist skills and passion to provide Art Workshops in different settings tailored to the need of the group or individuals. An idea I would develop over the next few years.

I have two beautiful children, trying to balance a full time role with two babies twenty-six months apart and splitting up with their father made me make the decision to go part time in my Council career and strive to make the business a success. Through consultations and meeting with the providers, I have been commissioned by, I have tailor made some exciting educational projects covering a diverse range of subjects.
My passion is to deliver Art Workshops to some of the most vulnerable young people you can work with. art can be used in so many ways, to relax the mind, start conversations on new subject matter and the young people can never be wrong in what they create as it's all their own work which they can take pride in and ownership of.

My business is split into two parts the face painting side started with me painting children in one of the youth clubs I worked in. Although I'm very arty it took a while to master the face painting in the beginning, and not going to lie I painted a few dodgy spidermen to start off with. It was by chance that I changed to the world of adult face painting after being asked to take some neon face paints to a night out in Liverpool. The queue to add a bit of sparkle and face painting magic to a group of over thirty year olds, enjoying an old school rave was phenomenal. Hence the switch from children to adults. This side of the business now became a perfect combination of dance music and body paint.

Growing up in Liverpool, as well as travelling to surrounding cities in the 90's we got to experience some of the best night clubs and raves in the country, and fortunately for us ageing ravers and a second generation of followers, nights and festivals built around this music genre are organised by some of the most talented DJs and promoters. The greatest part for me these ravers love a bit of sparkle.

The last five years have been one big adventure, the buzz you get working on big events and being creative in your work, meeting new people and talking to people of all ages who share your love for music makes you love every minute you work.

Setting your own business up isn't easy and after five years I'm still learning new artistic methods and skills to help me grow professionally. I want to continue to grow the business in both areas to provide the best life possible for me and my two children. I am lucky to have a fantastic mother on hand for late night babysitting as the events I work on certainly don't finish early. The recent pandemic has virtually written the last year off business wise, but what I am grateful for is the magical time it has given me to be creative with the children at home and come up with new ideas for when life becomes normal again.

I have spent weeks tearing my hair out wondering whether to give it all up and go back to a full time career, but small projects I have delivered during lockdown safely, have received such positive feedback that it has started to set aside the worry. I have kept to the decision to continue next year with ideas I have managed to develop with all this free time. I am feeling confident and positive enough to say that the future will make Ginger Island its most successful yet.

I feel one of the most important things we can do as women in business is encourage, support and empower others to become successful in their own right. As well as being, or becoming successful empowering others can become one of your greatest achievements. Its a beautiful thing to be able to work with young people supporting them into following their dreams no matter what life has thrown at them. With positivity and encouragement we can achieve anything.

"I trust that everything happens for a reason, even if we are not wise enough to see it."

———

OPRAH WINFREY

Chapter 11

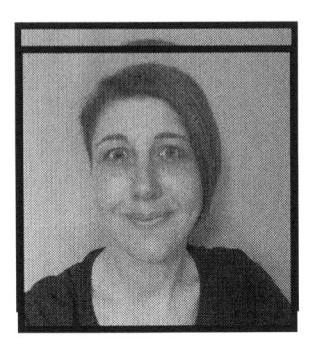

from Rock Bottom to Rocking It

Edwina Clark

Edwina is passionate about supporting and empowering women to be unashamedly themselves. She runs an online inclusive community where women can speak openly about the struggles they face without fear of judgement. They have regular guest speakers in to share their own journeys and share their knowledge with everyone there. She also uses this group to share her love of the same natural products that changed her life, enabled her to lose almost 80lbs and triggered a journey of recovery, self-discovery and self-worth.

With fellow author Becca Bryant, she co-runs a group for network marketers in any company, where ladies share their passion for using their businesses to help people rather than to simply provide an income. They share 'better ways' of growing a business that attracts customers.

@theedwinac
Facebook Group: Ed's Online Positivity Cafe
Facebook Group: MLM Hang Out

In 2014 I thought I was starting a new life. Having spent all of my adult existence in a very toxic relationship, getting the man I was married to out of our house had been hard enough, but living in a small seaside town meant he was never far away. He had chosen a life of substance misuse and violence over his own family, and each weekend he would show up intoxicated and remind us of this.

One Friday as I counted down the hours till he would come banging on the door again I was finally at the point where enough was enough. I packed me and the kiddies into the car and we moved eighty miles away for a fresh start. I thought this was going to be the start of something amazing, not realising the struggles that would come next. A decade of living through horrendous financial, emotional, physical and even worse abuse was over. I thought it would be like a fairy-tale, but this wasn't the case.

Shortly after moving I secured a permanent full time job in the profession my degree was in. This was my first 'proper job' as I perceived it. My kids started in their new school. Everything seemed to be falling into place; life was good, for a while. Then the past started to haunt us. A nasty court battle ensued over access to the children and this took its toll on me. Whilst the court's decision went in my favour in respect to my children, I was left to deal with the effects this had on them, a daughter who despised her father and a son who desperately missed him. I tried to get support for them but unfortunately this didn't come. I was left to manage it as best I could with minimal help from their school and no professional involvement.

I was also battling with my own health, both physically and mentally. Doctors' visits and hospital appointments became a regular occurrence; chronic condition after chronic condition was diagnosed; Crohn's Disease, Rheumatoid Arthritis, Fibromyalgia, Chronic Fatigue, Anxiety, Depression, the list goes on. Labels were being attached too, some by others and some looking back were perhaps self-imposed. With each new diagnosis came new prescriptions and the list of medications I was taking on a daily basis to function grew and grew.

Over the next few years I withdrew more and more. I was spiralling and I didn't know how to stop my fall. My mental health was the worst it had ever been, even worse than when I was with what I can I only describe as 'the monster'.

The strain of it all become too much. By 2018 I was off work on long term sick. I was taking thirty-seven pills a day just to function. My life wasn't a life at all, I just existed. I had two children who depended on me so I had to keep going, but every day was a struggle. It got to the point where I was barely functioning as a human being, spending my days (and nights) laid on the sofa, forgetting to eat or drink even, just staring into space or getting lost in the scroll hole of Facebook. Whilst I would never advocate for wasting your time jumping from one video to another on social media, for me one video I came across saved me.

I came across a video about a coffee, and the crazy lady promoting it really amused me. The product sounded too good to be true, but the lady talking about it was entertaining and she had grabbed my attention. She was happy, confident and outgoing, everything I wanted to be. So I watched her, almost stalked her, and hung onto her words. Whilst I didn't believe much of what she was saying, I was still transfixed by her.

In the end I agreed to try the product she kept talking about, but in my mind this was only to prove her wrong. A trial pack arrived through my letterbox. I had three days to see what all the fuss was about and three days to prove the product didn't work, especially for people like me. Instead I was the one who was wrong. In those three days I felt more positive, I got my sorry butt of the sofa, and I had lost 2lbs. This all seemed too much like a coincidence for me. I mean who would expect this from just switching my morning coffee. But coincidence or not I felt I had to give it a longer trial so I signed up for more.

I was desperate for some relief from the mess I felt my life was in and from the symptoms of my growing list of illnesses. It had a full money back guarantee, so with zero expectations I thought I would have three weeks of trying it, and then get my refund when it didn't work as advertised. Again I was wrong. That whole month was incredible. I felt alive again. I had energy, I had motivation and I had a part of me back. I returned to work too!

But then life threw me another curve ball, and I couldn't afford my 'monthly fix'. I was desperate to continue with the product, but when the choice is a pot of coffee or uniform for your ever-growing children, there is no choice really.

A few months later, back sick and desperate, I decided to join the business. I had no experience, but I had passion. I had determination. So I set about learning all I could about business and online selling as I needed to make this work.

The more I learned, the more I wanted to learn.

The more I helped people, the more people were attracted to me.

The more I shared my results and then the results of my customers, the more I wanted to reach more people.

It became addictive almost, I would wake up to messages from people who either wanted help or wanted to know more. I was so excited about it all that I bounced out of bed (yes I had gone back to sleeping in my own bed). This was an excitement I'd not felt before. I realised what I had at my fingertips, a golden ticket that could help others, and I loved it!

I rebranded once I realised just where my passion lay and who I most wanted to help. I began to connect with more and more women and set up 'Exhausted Mums Unite' on both Facebook and Instagram. I now have a community of over twelve hundred ladies (many of which are not mums) in my Facebook group too, which is a safe place where everyone can be unashamedly themselves and speak openly about the challenges that face us as women in today's world. This has been a particularly useful resource too many in the uncertain times that the pandemic of 2020 has brought us. It feels an honour to facilitate such a supportive environment where the fear of judgement has been removed.

Now I am not saying the products I sell will help everyone, they won't fix everything. But for me they were incredible and life changing, in part due to transformation that they triggered. I feel they were the catalyst to almost a new me being born. That may sound like a cliché, but those who followed my journey saw it unfold before their eyes.

The weight started to drop off me, 40lbs in the first three months. Whilst I in no way believe that weight and size should affect happiness, I was desperately unhappy in my own skin. I had gone way over the 200lbs mark and the steroids I relied on daily had not helped with this either. Due to my chronic conditions and my lack of actual movement, exercise was not a real possibility. I had tried most weight loss products and failed miserably, spending hundreds if not thousands of pounds for no results. Now I had something that was working for me, without the need to diet or replace meals. In total I have lost almost 80lbs, a huge physical change that people witnessed me sharing online.

But by far more important to me was the improvements in my health that came about. With careful consideration and in consultation with medical professionals (who didn't always agree), I reduced the medications I was taking, until I came off them completely. Physically and mentally I became a stronger person. I was able to be a 'proper' mum again. I finally had a life, not an existence. Through joining a network marketing business which most people perceive as a 'scam' I have grown hugely as a person. I have gone from rock bottom to supporting communities of thousands across Facebook.

Eventually I plucked up the courage to speak with people about the business aspect of what I do too. At first I found this hard, because I had no faith in myself as a leader but I was lucky that the low sign up cost and the very appealing pay structure helped me there. Plus it turned out I am a better leader than I realised and I needn't have worried or waited quite so long. I have now built a team who are building their own teams too, but we remain as one group, growing and learning together.

I have spoken to women across the globe about how from a past of shame and self-loathing I have gone on to build a business on the back of trying a product to prove someone wrong. The product triggered lots of changes in my health, but far greater than that was the change in me. Looking back I feel that it was a series of smaller things that each contributed to my rise. I am a huge believer in that our greatest glory does not come from never failing; it comes from how we rise each time, stronger and wiser.

I feel the growth of my business has come down to a few main factors, with lots of smaller elements along the way. I would love everyone to have the successes that I have and more, which is why as well as my own community group I also co-run a group on Facebook for network marketers who want to grow their business using attraction marketing rather than 'old school spammy snail' methods. The MLM Hang Out was born on the 5th of July 2019 and it continues to grow daily supporting over 1500 network marketers in all industries. This joint venture with Becca Bryant would never have happened had I not joined the company I am with and set about networking. It is strange to think that without that first conversation about dogs (one passion we both have in common) my life would be rather different now. This was another part of my journey that seemed quite small at the time, but Becca has since become my business partner, accountability buddy, but most importantly my biggest cheerleader and best friend.

I am also a networking leader for Mums In Business International (MIBI), a global female support and empowerment company, because my passion is to support as many women as possible, in as many ways as I can. In my own business and community I empower them with their health and wellbeing, in MIBI I support them in growing their business and I host child friendly networking events to assist them with this. This opportunity has opened new doors for me in my business and led to me meeting incredible and inspiring women such as Leona Burton, who continues to support me to 'kick ass' in all that I do.

My top tip to others in business is to get yourself out into the world. Whilst it can be a scary place, it is also full of supportive people who would love to be a part of your journey, you just need to find them, or let them find you. In February 2019 I sent a message that now makes people laugh, "I can't run a group and I am never doing a live". I honestly believed this when I sent it, because I had no confidence and very little knowledge. If someone had said to me two years ago that I would go on to do lives on Facebook I would I have laughed at them. I certainly would never have believed that I would be brave enough to share my story with anyone. I believed my past was something to be ashamed of and a secret that shouldn't be told.

I now do regular lives in my own groups as well as guest spots for other people's communities. I have been welcomed by hundreds of other women and asked to share my story to inspire others. I still feel the fear, my palms get sweaty, I feel the self-doubt creeping in at times, but I go ahead and do it anyway, because if each live inspires one person to make a change or 'go for it' in their own life/business, then it was worth every ounce of worry. I still make mistakes, get my words muddled, but honestly nobody minds because this is real life and it happens. If you are real, raw, even vulnerable, people will respect and love you for that. In fact this is how I came across this opportunity to write in this book, it would not have happened had I not have been getting myself out into the world and sharing my experiences with others.

No matter where you are sat reading this, no matter what stage you are at in your life, please just know this ... you can't change the past, but you damn sure can change your future. It might not be easy, but not much in life really is and your struggles today are building you stronger for tomorrow. Time will pass anyway, so you can either choose to spend it creating the life you want, or you will be forced to spend it living a life you don't want.

You've something I didn't have when I first started my new life, you have a cheerleader, you only need to reach out, you have me.

Edwina x

"The thing everyone should realize is that the key to happiness is being happy by yourself and for yourself."

ELLEN DEGENERES

Chapter 12

Unstoppable Introvert

Sammie Byrne

Sammie is a multi passionate business owner - which means she has way too many ideas and struggles sometimes to choose one thing!

She helps other women in business to get their business seen more, even if they prefer to stay behind the scenes themselves. This is something that has been part of her own business journey, which you'll read about in this chapter.

Facebook: @heysammieb
Facebook Group: The Introvert Success Lounge
Instagram: @heysammieb @unstoppableintrovert

www.sammieb.co.uk

I never thought that this is how this chapter would go, and I don't actually mean the chapter of this book. I never thought my business would have come full circle and link up to anything that happened when I was younger, and that this chapter of my life would be looking like this.

I'm Sammie Byrne and at the time of writing this book, I've completely overhauled my business, in the midst of the COVID-19 pandemic. My new direction is helping shy and introvert business owners to stand out online and get their business seen more, without having to be the centre of attention.

For years, I struggled with exactly this, but let's rewind a little to how things used to be before I even got into business ....

I grew up in North Devon, and to be honest I was really happy to leave when it was my time to go off to university. It's not that I couldn't wait to get away from Devon, in fact sometimes I miss living by the coast, but I was quite happy to have the chance to reinvent myself. I didn't have a particularly hard time at school, but I was never in the popular crowd. I did my own thing, had a few close friends, but not in the way that I see some others swanning off on girls holidays or still being a close knit group into their twenties and thirties. I just kept my head down, I was good academically and I got good exam results. But I was quiet, and in many situations I was pretty shy. I can see now that it held me back, and I let a lot of opportunities pass me by until well into my college and university time, because they would have been too far out of my comfort zone.

Drama class was the worst part of my school life. In fact, the feeling that I would get when I had to go into that class, was probably worse than most of the other things I've had to go through. Even worse than the feeling I had when I found I was pregnant and realised that would mean I had to have a blood test, and if you know me well then you'll understand that's saying something!

That experience at school sparked something in me to run my business in the way that I do today. I never want to have to be making up excuses to not do things. I want to run my business in a way that's enjoyable for me, otherwise I would just get a JOB and answer to someone else.

In November 2008, when I was in my mid twenties, after spending about ten years working in the restaurant management world, I decided I wanted a little side job for some extra money. What happened next, was probably the last thing anyone saw coming.

In December 2008, I did my first home party as an organiser with Ann Summers, and in April 2009 was promoted to a leader after building a team and having pretty good sales. What? Ann Summers? Standing in people's homes and talking in front of them about adult products? I can't really believe it myself still when I reflect back on it. I recall the reaction from my mum, I had gone upstairs onto her computer to have a look online and see what was involved in becoming a rep for Virgin Vie, which sold beauty products. So you can imagine her surprise when I came back to say that I had submitted my details to do something that was a million miles away from that.

That first party I did, I was terrified. I remember calling my, now husband, and telling him that it was like I was driving through a film set ready to get to the scary part of the movie. It was the middle of winter, I was driving down country lanes in the dark, no idea where I was going or who was going to be at this party. I'm not even sure I would be so brave now, to go into the houses of strangers!

Somehow, quite miraculously, I was good at this new venture.

Maybe my years working with horrible customers that wanted to send back their cold meals or hadn't got what they ordered had toughened me up and made me more confident. Or perhaps it was the testing relationships I had been in, including one that involved me flying solo to Albania multiple times to make sure my then boyfriend could get a visa to stay in the country, and another that saw all my rent money being gambled away by a man I had chosen to move in with. When I look back on these 'excellent' life choices, I cringe a little. But in all honesty I wouldn't be where I am now if it wasn't for all these experiences.

So something had definitely changed in me by the time I was spending my weekends at girly nights in and hen parties. I didn't feel so scared anymore. I was able to speak to people I didn't know, and stand up in front of a group of people and sell to them. Something I would never have thought would be my job. I was able to recruit and train others and manage a large team too.

However, there were still things I didn't want to do, that were being drummed into me as the 'done thing'. Calling everyone I know to see if they want a party? No thank you. Going into one of my local stores for a couple of hours and chatting to the customers as they were browsing? Not happening. Knocking on the doors of people that lived in my area? No way.

I didn't feel I could force my team to do these things either and this became a bit of a stumbling block for me and created massive resistance. Eventually it led to me moving on to something else, and this became a bit of a pattern. When I felt like I had to be something I wasn't in order to be successful, I would move on to something else, in the hope that this would be the thing that I could do on my own terms. Funnily enough, it never was.

Overall I spent ten years in network marketing companies, with various different types of products. I won awards, achieved company holidays, got to travel to the US and made some amazing friends over the years. But I have never been able to do lots of the things others do, and that mainly came down to what I felt that other people would think of me. Live video on Facebook made an appearance mid way through my network marketing career and I never wanted to do it. I recall doing one video on Periscope to announce a winner of a team competition, it was about forty-five seconds long and I hated it so much that I vowed not to do that again!

I still managed to have a successful business though. I still managed to build large teams, I still hit promotions and won incentives. I just wanted more, I knew that I was holding myself back. I was always comparing myself to others and it wasn't helping to get me where I wanted to be.

This brings me to where I am today, I had been working as a brand designer for the last few years and something I love to talk about is how to stand out from the crowd online. One of the things I found from my Facebook group members was that making THEMSELVES visible was a real struggle. Making videos, taking selfies, talking about their lives, or maybe going to in person events. They feel stuck in their business because they can't figure out what they can do instead. They would prefer to just stay behind the scenes, behind the computer screen where it's safe and not scary. This is of course, just how I used to feel (and still do sometimes).

I strongly believe that we get into business to enjoy it, and to not stress, and whilst pushing ourselves a bit out of our comfort zone is great, we don't need to do all the things that absolutely terrify us to the point of just doing nothing at all. Why should we have to do things just because everyone else is? Why are we made to feel so much pressure to conform to other people's ideas of there only being one route to success? Once we let go of that idea, we have more freedom to build the business we want to. It's like someone has granted us the permission to just relax, and take the pressure off.

One of the things that I'm really conscious of, is that I don't want my daughter to grow up feeling like she has to do things a certain way in order to see success. Not that I think that will be an issue, she's only four and she's already one of the most headstrong people I know! This doesn't always make life easy, we've had our fair share of difficulties in trying to juggle life and business. Business has often had to take the back seat as it's been a lot harder than I ever thought it would be, to do both.

During the lockdown period of the Covid-19 pandemic, my new business direction begun. Bespoke design work was impossible whilst working from home with a preschooler who couldn't go and run off her energy at the soft play centre, our usual activity of choice. I also realised that I had a much bigger message to share, rather than simply how to make someone's business look good. I wanted to show other women in business, who had the same struggles that I did when I started my business, that there is no cookie cutter way to do business, and that other people's 'rules' for success were not the only way.

I'm an ideas person so I love to help come up with something that will make another business owner stand out and get noticed, by doing things their way. Doing things in a way that plays to their inner super strengths and creates a business that they really really love.

I believe that shy and introvert people can have successful businesses too, and I'm on a mission to show how it can be done! At the time of writing this, I am about to launch a brand new podcast, something I would NEVER have thought about doing. I would love to see the reaction of some of my old school friends, particularly as one comment has always stuck in my mind for over twenty years, that I would probably not end up doing anything more exciting than working in a restaurant.

It's amazing the things that fuel you, and make you want to push yourself forward, how seemingly insignificant comments can stick with you. Other things that I want my daughter to know are; you can be anything you want to be, regardless of what anyone else says, and to always think about what you are telling yourself and others, as words can stay with someone for a long time.

Here's to getting further out of the old comfort zone!

"Don't be intimated by what you don't know. That can be your greatest strength and ensure that you do things differently from everyone else."

SARAH BLAKELY

Chapter 13

It Just Makes Scents

Lisa Haythorne

Mother, sister, aunt, daughter, friend, partner and business owner. Who knew you could have so many titles and rock it?
It's not easy, and life defines you, creates you and berates you. It's how you use it that makes the difference.

Here's a little glimpse into Lisa's life, the things she has overcome and how she got to where she is now, even on those days where giving up appears easier. Don't, you've got this!

www.lisashomefragrances.com

Instagram: @lisashomefragrances
Facebook: @lisashomefragrances

I'm a twenty-eight year old small business owner from Doncaster. I've been in business for two and a half years and I've never found myself to be happier or more enthusiastic about the next steps than I have now I actually believe in myself. Believing in yourself is the hardest thing to do when you've spent your life in a shadow of doubt. Learning to believe in myself hasn't been easy, in fact it took the words of strangers to enable me to overcome my own barriers set by not knowing my worth, or valuing myself.

There are many reasons I embarked on my journey into being a self made entrepreneur. My school life and the challenges I faced, my anxiety, my children and my health. It hasn't been easy but it has made me!

At school I was an extrovert, I had vibrant multi coloured hair, I would wear what I wanted and beamed confidence. I was the girl to sort your problems out, I could always see the bright side, the silver lining. But that was just what people saw. Inside I was a broken little girl, crying out to be saved. I was bullied. For a very long time I was bullied and ridiculed by a girl and her friend. I developed an eating disorder, I calorie counted and exercised until I couldn't breathe. I felt I had to prove to them I wasn't what they were saying about me. No one knew about it, because hey I'm the girl with bright pink hair, I'm fine right... Wrong.

One day whilst lining up at school the girl and her friends began pushing me, calling me names and suggesting I needed surgery to fix my body. I lashed out and hit my bully. Albeit the wrong thing to do, I was thirteen years old and at breaking point. The girl's family had me arrested, despite the police themselves saying it was a playground issue. Not only that, I was expelled from school for a month. I was isolated, alone and felt that maybe there was something wrong with me, maybe she had been right. By this point I had body dysmorphia.

I wasn't loud anymore, I wasn't me anymore. I returned to school to find they had took me out of every single class and moved me into another group, away from all my friends. Isolated further by a system that allowed me to be penalised for being a victim.

So I stopped going to school after that. I taught myself at home and attended my exams. I passed them all with five Bs and seven Cs. I was proud of my achievements without their help.

I spent a lot of time mulling over what I wanted to do when I 'grew up' from singer to forensic scientist and everything in between. I chose psychiatry. I wanted to help people, like me, who had mental health differences, that needed help to understand themselves and the world we live in.

I changed schools and began my AS Levels. I didn't realise how bad my anxiety was at this point. I would go to class and then hide in the toilet. I ate my dinner in the toilet, I never made any friends. I was even given a 'buddy' to try and help me mix with people. This didn't work. My anxiety won and by the end of the year I had 18% attendance. Albeit I still passed my exams, but I could have done better. It wasn't enough to get me into university.

I had to have a word with myself, think of the future. Convince myself to get past this fear of people, the fear of being judged. And so I enrolled at Doncaster college to study health and social care. I still wanted to help people. I was shy and nervous and on my first day, I felt my whole body sweat as I arrived late to the first class. There I was stood in front of a whole class of people and I had to pick where to sit. I looked around and there was a table of four girls that stood out to me, I sat with them. For two years they were the best group of friends, with a few more girls added along the way, I started to feel happier, I enjoyed going to college.

I even attended summer school, where I was awarded head girl for overcoming my fears in the three days I'd been there. I'd began on the nursing summer school, but I didn't want to be a nurse and asked to swap. I left my friends in nursing and pursued the psychology school. It was amazing.

At the end of the trip when I stood there being awarded for being me, it finally hit home. I am amazing but I am human. I let others destroy my image of myself, a true victim of imposter syndrome.

After eight years in education, all the facts I had learned along the way and the challenges I faced. I finally left with another qualification under my belt, at a triple distinction grade two.

My health:

At age thirteen, I developed unexplained abdominal pain. I was doubled over, couldn't move and was rushed to the doctors. No one could understand it and I was sent away. Returning to the doctors almost daily with this pain in my lower abdomen I was eventually sent for a scan. Nothing. They couldn't find anything wrong with me. I was again sent away, told I had to live with it.

I spent the duration of my school life in agony. But when I started college my friend 'Alice' also had problems. So together we began visiting the hospital. This was five or six years after the pain began.

Multiple doses of antibiotics and nothing had changed. So I eventually got sent for further scans. They found my left ovary had decided to double in size, for no apparent reason. Again, I was sent away, it would get better on its own they said. It didn't.

At nineteen years old I fell pregnant with my first child. It was a difficult pregnancy with me developing severe sickness, I was hospitalised a few times with dehydration. My pregnancy was so hard for me, mentally and physically. Towards the end of the pregnancy we discovered my baby was breech, with her head happily jammed in my ribs. It was too late to turn her and I was booked in for a cesarean section.
Recovering from the section itself was very difficult, painful and took a long time. I had developed problems with my lower pelvic area. I had experienced pain, discomfort and uterine bleeding for three consecutive years. I tried various birth control options and nothing helped me. The doctors would send me on my way.

When I fell pregnant with my second child, my pregnancy was awful. We had so many complications, hospital trips and more. We didn't know way would happen, I had an area of bleeding on my womb the size of a tennis ball. I was weak, I was in pain and I was scared.

A planned cesarean was put in place but I went into labour early. A very traumatic labour and life changing. I saw the clock on the wall stop and go back in time, it sounds silly but something saved us that night. Things could have been so different. My girls could have lost their mum. It was terrible, after surgery when I awoke I felt lost, scared and relieved all at the same time. I'd suffered with postnatal depression since my first pregnancy, but I came out of my second feeling worse than before. I think the confusion in my mind over everything that happened exacerbated my low mood along side the pain I was in. Being told I could have died was unbelievable, and being told if I got pregnant again I'd likely die was a huge slap in the face.

I was in pain every day, with emotions all over the place and still the doctors would tell me there's nothing they could do. A few pain killers a year and off I went. Learning to live with this pain that's haunted me for years.

When I fell pregnant with my youngest I was terrified, I thought I was going to leave my girls. And like magic my pregnancy was a walk in the park. I had nine months of bliss my pain wasn't as bad during this pregnancy and I loved it. But I didn't embrace it because of the fears.

I had to have a third cesarean due to the weakness in my abdomen but also had to have my tubes cut and cauterised to prevent any further pregnancies. I was awake for the surgery.

As I laid there being operated on the surgeon pulled the sheet down and said 'when did you have an ectopic pregnancy?'

I didn't know I'd had an ectopic pregnancy. But damage done to my tubes shows I did. I'm in that much pain, all the time that I didn't even realise I'd been through another life threatening situation and came out the other side.

It wasn't just the ectopic I'd discovered either. I had to have a bowel specialist come to separate my bowel from my left ovary. They had become bound by scar tissue. Something I later learned to be the cause of most of my pain.

Recovery was difficult, my organs had been moved around and cut apart. I spent weeks slowly shuffling around the house. I couldn't use the stairs, I slept on the sofa with my partner sleeping on the floor. It was a strain on the whole family. My youngest is my phoenix, the child I never thought I could have, my blessing. I felt completely different, my depression hadn't gone but it wasn't stopping me anymore. I was happy. In pain but happy and that's how I've been since.

My pain has been the biggest inhibitor. Following the birth of my youngest, I fought for eighteen months to get a referral to a specialist because a scan and MRI had shown confounding things.

I had a laparoscopy in December 2018. I found that my organs are all stuck together with scar tissue. I was in surgery for six hours having the scar tissue removed. They removed as much as they could do safely but left me with a lot of scar tissue.

My body's healing method is to generate scar tissue. Every time I do something that pulls on my stomach, more scar tissue develops, making my pain worse. My surgeon agreed to a hysterectomy to try and eliminate some of my pain. However, with the covid 19 situation, I have had my operation postponed. But I hope to have a little less pain once the surgery is done.

Being in pain for over half my life is one of the main reasons I wanted to start my own business as well as working around being a full time mummy. Some days I can't move, other days I'm able to move but with pain. Working for myself from home enables me to do what I can when I can.

My Business:

Lisa's Home Fragrances is my saviour. A hobby I love turned into a business that has so much prospective. My business began with a bag of wax, four or five fragrances and dream of succeeding. It was my twenty-sixth birthday, I wanted to achieve something, I wanted to break the chain so to speak. I wanted to feel like more than 'just a mum' as many of us can feel from time to time. We're approaching three years in business and I am so proud.

I make a variety of home fragrance products, specialising in wax melts. I also make room sprays, reed diffusers and more. I currently have sixty fragrances in my collection and it grows by the day.

I pride myself on providing high quality products at affordable prices. Luxury shouldn't cost the earth, we all deserve a little luxury in life.
Working from home allows me to spend time with my girls, work when I feel able and enjoy life as much as I can. On the days where I can't move through the pain use my social media platforms, to promote and advertise products and on the days where I am feeling better I work wonders creating little pieces of magic to lavish your home with lush aromas. I work around me and it's the best thing I've ever done.

I have a product in the works that will change the way we treat our sportswear and gym bags. In line with this, We have a sponsorship deal with a team GB combat sambist. Ewan Jack 'the gripper' Lister, A coach at Doncaster sambo gym, a very active local MMA fighter who regularly competes, is a friend of myself but also of the business. He has a love of our lemon sherbet. An incredible scent if I do say so myself.

My journey is far from over I have so much to come and more ideas developing every day. I still face challenges, I've had financial issues, health issues and I work around my children, school runs and trips. Life is hectic but I wouldn't have any other way. I'm excited about what I have to come and the challenges I may face along the way.

I don't see a challenge as something stopping me, I see it as an adjustment, a way for me to change or develop to overcome or adapt anything that tries to get in my way.

Life can be hard, it throws things at us that we least expect but it's all part of the journey. The journey can take many turns, you may fail but you will always get back up. Believe in yourself you are your best asset.

I've experienced Isolation, loneliness, depression, anxiety and more. I look back now and I'm grateful for each and every challenge, for they set up my journey to success. They made me who I am. The good, the bad, the ugly, its all educated me and lead me onto a path I know in my heart Is my future.

I am Lisa. Successful business owner, crafter, mother, partner, chronic pain warrior but most of all, I am me!

One thing I always suggest to people is to listen to 'Baz Lurhman always wear sunscreen'. I heard it when I was younger and it truly changed the way I thought. Especially the part in the speech / song where it states some people at age 40 still don't know what they want to do with their life. What might be right now, might not be in the future. Our journey isn't set. Try not to worry about where you'll end up, focus on how you're going to get there. The journey is fun.

Be social, as hard as it can be sometimes, especially if you have a phobia of putting yourself out there. I still struggle, but I keep trying to be me for all to see. People like you as well as your business.

Mainly, don't let others experiences affect your future decisions. What works for you may not work for others and vice versa.

You've got this!!

Lisa

"A woman's best protection is money of her own"

———

CLARE BOOTHE LUCE

Chapter 14

Learning to Bloom

Louisa Herridge

Louisa is an English teacher and Relax Kids mindfulness coach delivering mindfulness and wellbeing classes both on Zoom and in the Warrington area in schools and nurseries.

Blooming Daffodils is a new and exciting family well-being business with the purpose of supporting families to learn how to connect with their emotions and feelings using mindfulness and relaxation techniques. Louisa is passionate about supporting mums and their children who have experienced trauma.

Facebook: @relaxkidswithlouisa @bloomingdaffodils
Twitter @bloom_daffodils
Instagram @relaxkids_louisa
BLOG: www.lou15a.Wordpress.com
Website: www.relaxkids.com

My story of growth and rebirth as a Relax Kids Coach. Starting a business from the depths of despair and coming through as a Blooming Daffodil.

The hand came from nowhere. An outstretched arm with bulging veins. It was him - bursting through the door like a raging bull. Before she could catch a breath, the vice like hand gripped her throat; her head thrust against the wall. In that moment her life stood still. The sands of time teetered on the edge; the world precariously on its axis as the magnitude of this moment was born. In that instant time changed. She changed. As a mindset coach she is committed to empowering women to change their mindset and and to learn tools to promote positive change in their lives.

"If you ever ignore me again, I will come around and repeatedly punch you in the face". His words spun in her mind like a record scratched and stuck. No one to reset the track, no one to stop the endless noise on repeat. Her daughter's cries echoed in the vacuum. The lioness inside her roared to protect her young, but in his grasp, she was a mouse, caught in the snatches of the hawk. He'd preyed on her; had tormented her and now she was caught.

He pulled her roughly - half wrestling, half floating she moved on air and was thrust into the depths of the sofa. His weight bore down; the blur of crying and shouts filled her head. Who was shouting? Was it her? Was it him? His claws tightened and her mouse like stature fought with all its might. Unwilling to relent but unable to fight. Two hands now tightened and pressed. He sweated and his eyes bulged as he lost all sense of his own being. Together they were lost. Her thoughts raced; her body fought. Spots of white danced across her eyes and the burning in her throat intensified. The burning to scream; burning to breathe; an inferno of pain to survive.

He pressed; he enjoyed her pain - the power. He pressed harder, she winced. *How dare she ignore him; she did this. Her. All her fault.* She was starting to resist the fight. He tightened his grip and the need for air heightened. He heard her gasp, felt her struggle… heard his daughter's pained cries. She was there. Mummy. Crying for Mummy. Screaming. The sands of time momentarily frozen for him. He heard his daughter cry. In that moment he realised he had lost. *She had done this; this was her fault.* He let go and ran. She pounced from the sofa; not a thought for her own life but that of her daughter; to protect her young. She held her close and wept a roar of anguish.

****

That was the day last year when my world spun on its axis. Life as I knew it changed. I was assaulted and strangled to the near point of passing out in my own home, by the father of my child. We'd been separated for a year but I'd tried to leave him for a long time prior to that. I had been a victim of Narcissistic abuse for six years - emotionally, mentally, verbally and physically. Yet as a strong, educated and confident woman it took another six months before I could fully say out loud that I was a victim of abuse. I am a victim of abuse.

When the police interviewed me and asked if he'd ever done anything like this before I said "No". Well he didn't hit me... so was it abuse? But what about the time he pushed me... grabbed my face... restrained my wrists... threw things at me? Yes, all of this and more. As the Police Officer asked probing questions, suddenly six years of abuse unfolded. Verbal abuse – calling me names, swearing at me, mocking me. Mental abuse... always making me believe things were my fault, twisting the truth, lying. Turns out he was quite the expert.

I had left him two years before the assault. Moved towns, jobs and started a new empowered life – or so I thought. At that point I knew the relationship was wrong and that I was sad more than I was happy – but Narcissistic abuse was not a term that I knew anything about. After a mere two months alone in my new world, I was dragged back into his web and this time I was caught even more tightly. I can see now that he used all the classic Narcissistic techniques – love bombing, future faking and as an expert at knowing my weaknesses he used them to his full advantage. Offering me a new and improved version of him and the life with him that I loved and so wanted to believe could be true.

Fairly quickly his mask slipped and the old ways resumed. This time it was worse. His abuse had started to impact on my daughter too. She had witnessed him verbally and aggressively abusing me. She saw the bruises after he'd shoved me over. I was lying to people about the bruises and that was when I knew. Finally, I made a full break. He moved out and this time it was for good!

Even though I'd physically broken free from him I was still very much controlled by him emotionally. He tried to control my life, using our daughter as a pawn in his game. My belief that my daughter needed to have her father in her life meant that I still continued to excuse and ignore his incredibly more volatile, irregular and controlling behaviour. Every meeting with him sent my anxiety higher and higher. His calls became more frequent, he would pop round unannounced; even let himself into my home when I wasn't there. He still had my key. It took me five months to drum up the courage to ask for the key back. My life was still treading on egg shells and I just didn't know how to escape from his grip.

Through support from special family and friends (you know who you are) I became stronger and tightened my boundaries and self-care. The more I protected myself and the more distance I put between us the more erratic he became as he lost more and more control. I could see him beginning to unravel as I found the strength to stand up to him. To make him leave my home when he was being abusive. To refuse to take his calls. All of this resulted in more abuse and bombardment of texts. The day he attacked me was because I had put the phone down on him when he was verbally abusing me the day before. This abuse continued on my driveway, in front our three-year-old. Trying to shut the door to keep him out of my house is what made him flip. Subsequently forcing his way into my home, grabbing me by the throat - holding me down on the sofa with his hands gripped like a vice around my throat and strangling me to the point that I was gasping for breath and was seeing white spots. I thought that I was going to die. Thankfully he let go. This happened in front of our innocent three-year-old daughter. She witnessed everything. In her words she saw Daddy hurt her beautiful Mamma and we have both every day since been through trauma, anxiety, nightmares, flashbacks. Both diagnosed with PTSD, life did literally change for us both in that instant.

I have had depression for many years. Looking back probably due to the abusive relationship that I was in. But it had always been labelled by him that I was crazy or needed my happy pills. I had been medicated for Post-natal depression, which I do not want to dismiss, but the fact that I was NOT allowed to stay in my pyjamas immediately after giving birth and was expected by him to be up and ready to be out and about (Kwik Fit for new tyres on day3?!) makes me look back with a different view to my very difficult first six weeks of being a new mum. With a supportive partner, or even on my own I may have a different story to tell.

Throughout the two years of trying to break free of him my anxiety and depression worsened. Medication was increased steadily and the aftermath of the attack is a blur. The assault was June 2019. I took nine days off work and then tried to get back to normal. Overnight I was a 24/7 single mummy with no shared contact and a very stressful, pressured full time teaching job with additional responsibilities and a looming OFSTED inspection. My GP warned me that if I didn't deal with IT things could get worse. I didn't have a clue how to deal with IT, so I made myself very busy having a lovely life and cracked on with work.

At the same time as running the *Mummy is Fine* show I was also dealing with court, solicitors, hearings. Facing him. I filed for a non-molestation and non-contact order which were granted. The first time I faced him was a week after. Face to Face in court. Our names tagged against each other. War of the Roses. He couldn't look at me. My stomach was in knots but I stared at him. He caught my eye – I stared until he looked away. I was strong and defiant on the outside but in my body and my head it was another story.

Sixth months later, two court appearances, OFSTED, Scarlet Fever and many other stresses I broke down. It was December, I was done. I could no longer cope with life as a single mummy, full time English teacher and an ongoing court case. My little one was also struggling with anxiety, nightmares, loss of her dad. I was mentally broken. How do you tell people how broken you are when on the outside you are smiling and confident? Every day I was faking life in work, with my friends. The dark fog was getting darker and the new enemy anxiety had taken over. Everyone knew I'd been assaulted but it was no longer spoken about, but it was all I could think about. Every waking and sleeping thought I was literally consumed by it. Sleep was no escape. Nightmares that I cannot even begin to repeat. Too harrowing to dream let along to try and remember. But all were linked to the attack, the fear, the anxiety. Even writing this now I feel like I have a size 12 boot standing on my chest. Tears stinging in my eyes as I try not to go back there.

The cracks became too deep and I broke down in tears in a lesson with some lovely pupils. Pupils on the corridor saw me crying in a morning on my way in to class. Hyperventilating in the car as I drove past his house, reliving the nightmare. I was having very dark thoughts. I wanted to sleep and for it all to go away. I wanted to lie back in the swimming pool and to be consumed by the water. The peace of the water throbbing in my ears taking away my thoughts. I wasn't well. A good friend said to me you won't realise how poorly you are until you look back. My work friends who saw me daily kept me going. I didn't want to give in, but eventually I was told I had to stop. I hadn't dealt with IT and here IT was stronger than ever.

Taking time away from work allowed me the time to spend more quality time with my little one. To do the school run, to meet other mums and to attend the Christmas service. As I listened to Away in a Manger I sobbed. I didn't think I would ever stop. I felt so guilty about all the things I had missed. I couldn't even take her on her first day at school. So being away from work allowed me to relish these simple, but so important milestones.

As I allowed myself time it was apparent that I needed extra support for myself and my daughter. I embarked on Counselling which became life changing. However, I'd struggled to get any help for my daughter via the NHS being told Sadly there is a gap in support for this age group. I was becoming more desperate and then I was recommended Relax Kids by a friend. I contacted the local Relax Kids coach hoping for a miracle and I found one!

I booked three one-to-one sessions with a lovely Relax Kids coach. She came highly recommended and when I'd spoken to her on the phone I felt so at ease. The first session honestly changed my life. Something special happened that day. It was January 2020, seven months after the attack and the class which was supposed to be for my little one actually helped me to start to deal with IT. During the class there is a FEEL section where we massaged each other. As we massaged each other I started to cry. Just a few tears. Then an almighty release came. I couldn't understand where it was coming from. I tried to shield the tears but a knowing smile made me know that I was safe and it was ok to show my emotion. After this was RELAX. We lay down together on the sofa with lavender filled blankets and we were still. At 12pm on a Saturday with a four old I was still. She read Aladdin's Magic Carpet and the Unicorn and I can still picture my magical unicorn soaring through the sky. We lay still and relaxed for twenty minutes! In our chaotic life filled with anxiety and pain we had never been so close and still. When the session finished and we were alone we both cried together, unsure as to why, we clung to each other and sobbed. It was a release that we both needed. In that moment I knew that Relax Kids was special.

From here I started to research Relax Kids and was thrilled to see the franchise opportunities. Sitting in a soft play centre I felt a real buzz of excitement as I read about the company and thought about how this could be the answer that I was looking for. In that moment I actually knew that I was going to go for it. My foggy brain couldn't quite work out how it was possible, but I knew that like the phoenix I had to rise from these ashes and that eventually I could come back stronger. But sadly, that was still a way off. I had the final court hearing to contend with and that was all consuming. I couldn't sleep with anxiety, but in my insomniac state the Relax Kids magic kept drawing me back. I must have read the information a thousand times. The escapism and the dream of a chance to work with and support other families like us was very much alive.

****

As she sat in the draughty court room her eyes were glued to the wooden table she was stiffly perched against. As she waited, she played with her ring, twisting it around – her comfort. She looked at the ring - a heart-shaped ring, a gift from a previous life. Valentine's Day. Another love-bomb. The ring - a declaration of love that she needed to know that he was the one. How ironic that now this ring - the ring that symbolised their love was still on her finger. The ring had become forgotten - another meaningless token of his facade. She'd only kept it as her finger felt naked without it and no replacement had yet found its way to her. So there it lay. A dormant reminder of their love. A dormant reminder of the grip that he had over her, yet ironically now it was her only comfort.

Only three seats away from him. He looked upset. Inside, her old psyche wanted to go to him to comfort him to believe that he was good inside. Fool. As his words came out and the same tone and spit of belligerence left his body, she recoiled - the old flutters of anxiety rose in her chest. She wanted to rip the ring from her finger and throw it. To make a dramatic metaphorical show of casting the last trace of him away.

As the judge spoke, his words whirled around her head. She couldn't focus. She clutched her scarf resting on her lap and twisted it tightly around her hand. The pain of the taut material against her skin was a reminder that this was real. He was there. She pulled the scarf tighter and tried hard to focus and to listen. She held onto the scarf and the reality of the pain, staring at the life lines in the wooden table beneath her hands. She imagined the life and growth of the tree that had been sacrificed. There she was a broken tree weathered from the storm of the last year. She imagined the tall tree growing and thriving and smiled to herself. She had to regrow. Her roots were there and this was going to be the end of one chapter and the beginning of another. She had the lines and wounds, internal injuries, tormented memories and nightmares of the storm that had been their lives together.

The Judge's words woke her from her daydream. 'Thirteen counts of abuse – FACT' 'No contact' 'Three-year non-molestation order.' She'd won. But this felt far from a victory.

She'd had eight months of freedom from him along with eight months of upset, pain and confusion. And now they were saying it was over. She had the outcome that she never thought possible. The face of her daughter was painted at the front of her mind. How was she going to tell her daughter and break her heart? There was no happiness to be taken from this ending. She had won and her daughter was protected. Yet in those final minutes she caught a glimpse of him and wanted to run to him. Seven years of abuse. Seven years of being the victim and now there she was - triumphant in court but the most empty and desperate inside that she had ever felt.

****

As I left the courtroom, I only just made it into the toilet before an intense guttural cry escaped my body. The cry reverberated around the old, echoey building. I have never cried like that before or since. Such a gut-wrenching cry of pain, relief, despair and disbelief. One that I hope never to experience again. It was over. I didn't have to face him again.

That date in February had haunted me since October. Four months living with a ticking time-tomb waiting to find out what lay ahead of us. I had never fully let myself imagine a life without him in it. All my energy was consumed with anxiety and worry. After the intense, all-consuming adrenaline of court and the final result I was deflated. A hopeless balloon with no life left. For the next week I was absent. I lay on the sofa for days and nights on end. Trapped in waking sleep and suffocated by my own thoughts. Only getting into some semblance of dress to do the school run. I was broken. IT had broken me.

Slowly I began to rebuild my strength (again) and thanks to my amazing counsellor I began to take control of my own vision and my own future. After being off work for two months something had shifted in me. The career driven teacher suddenly realised that it was okay to not be a full-time teacher with a responsibility, always striving for the next promotion, to be Outstanding. Sending my daughter to breakfast club and afterschool club, spending weekends and evenings marking. Hearing my daughter say You love marking more than me. Missing her assemblies and Harvest Festival the Phonics Meet and Great. Something shifted and I realised that I could still be career driven but I could change gear so that the speed of the drive suited the journey that I wanted to be on. I decided that I was going to train to be a Relax Kids Coach and go part time or on supply as a teacher. I was going to redirect my life. I registered for the training. Filled with drive I had my whole future mapped out. There was no stopping me!

Then Coronavirus hit and the world stopped!

My training was scheduled to be the day before lockdown. I didn't attend and I felt like my world had ended. My dream was over. Lockdown on top of missing out on the training sent me spiralling back into depression and anxiety. Coronavirus was taking away all of my plans and significantly my control. I was also due back at work on a phased return, I had requested part-time but nothing was guaranteed. I felt like the pipe dream had come to an end and I had to return to the rat-race.

As I tried desperately to drag myself out of the despair and depression of lockdown, I made another important decision to reignite my blog. I had previously written a blog during maternity, yet sadly when I returned to teaching it slipped. I often beat myself up about why I stopped writing, but the reason is, I was too scared to write. When I write emotion floods the page and my fingers go ahead of my brain. I was terrified to feel what was really happening in my life. The world around me had stopped spinning, I was off the treadmill and there were no more excuses. My previous blog, The Little Book of Sick was my salvation during maternity leave and suddenly I was back in an all familiar place of isolation and desperation and I needed to write.

It was a sunny spring day and as I mused about the blog, a soul daffodil was growing in our garden. It always amazes me each spring when these delicate golden trumpets are able to recover from the icy ground and bloom back to life. On our daily lockdown walks we were surrounded by beautiful daffodils and after rescuing two trampled daffodils and placing them in my sunny kitchen window, the name Blooming Daffodils was born. We had survived the depths of cold and pain and were now ready to step back into the sunshine to bloom.

As I started to write, my anxiety rocketed as I put my thoughts and feelings back out on a public platform. I kept going and having all but given up on Relax Kids becoming a reality I was given a purple ray of hope. The wonderful Marneta Viegas, founder of Relax Kids and team at Relax Kids HQ had very quickly, but very professionally designed an online training programme. I still had to wait several weeks and was like an impatient child at Christmas but finally I was able to train. I am honoured that I was in the first ever cohort of online trainees. I completed my training during at home, whilst home schooling and virtually teaching and it brought me back to life. I learned so much more about the magic of Relax Kids for children and parents. The more I learned about the company and the wonderful seven-step programme the more I realised how crucial Relax Kids is.

So, what is Relax Kids? Relax Kids is literally that. It is a class that promotes mindfulness to relax children using a combination of movement, games, stretching, massage, breathing, positive affirmations and visualisation. The sessions begin with high energy activities and take the children on a Magical Adventure which ends with twenty lovely minutes of calm relaxation. And it REALLY works!

During Lockdown we were both having severe nightmares. My little girl's night terrors were awful. Her attachment to me was so severe and her PTSD meant that she couldn't bear me being alone downstairs. Her teacher had bought her a worry monster. Reading her worries made me weep. I worry that my Daddy will hurt Mummy. A bad man will take Mummy away. The bed time routine had become so stressful that we would both be in tears as she would beg me to Take the bad thing away. Make the bad dreams stop. I'm scared of the monsters and daddy.

Whilst waiting to complete the training I ordered the Relax Kids books and 'had a go' at using the techniques that we'd been taught in our earlier sessions. For weeks she had cried and screamed in her sleep. The first night that we read the Visualisations she went to sleep calmly after the second story. A week later and it was still working. We both slept so much better and this is where our recovery truly began. Steadily her nightmares decreased and I now have my little girl back who loves bedtime and we enjoy so many magical adventures together. Of course, PTSD never fully goes away but at five years old she is able to self-regulate, to control her breathing and to re-focus herself when the bad dreams come. This is the true Magic of Relax Kids and I was desperate to share it with others.

Back in early March I had held several meetings with other business women that I know and I had a really good action plan ready to go of places that I could run my sessions - schools and nurseries to approach – sports clubs, café bars. And then the world stopped. Completing the training was one thing - but how on earth could I make this business work without any kids? God bless Zoom! It was the saviour of Lockdown in so many ways and has enabled me to fully launch my business from home! Lockdown was in fact the perfect time to launch as the aim of the company is Creating Calm, Confident Children in Chaotic times! And at this time, it was more needed than ever.

I completed my sample classes via Zoom and socially distanced when it was possible and by July, I was fully qualified. I launched my first chargeable online Zoom JUST RELAX class for adults and had the most fun. I offered the classes to Mums first of all as I wanted to share the magic and help others mums to see how important it is to focus time on ourselves and demonstrate how the skills can help their children. I am now on Course Number three and have repeat business. Ladies who beg me to run classes as it is their only hour to themselves a week! 'Absolutely magical. - Within a few minutes I had completely forgotten about my worries and at the end felt completely relaxed.' (Just Relax participant)

The first Magical Adventure's Kids class was with my daughter and our neighbours' twins on my front lawn. My daughter was AWFUL. She refused to join in and purposely tried to upset the class and even mocked me. I was mortified. Somehow the twins managed to engage and despite several toilet stops we got through the class and by the end I was so relieved as they relaxed and were excited to collect their certificates. From here I pushed forward and delivered an online Zoom to fifteen Reception Children: Note to self – limit groups to six children! My confidence grew and grew as I delivered more 'freebie' classes in order to complete my certificate.

When I saw a plea on Facebook for a Mum looking for ways to support her anxious son, I got in touch. Boom! I had my first PAID one-to-one booking! It was via Zoom and for a very anxious child. As soon as these sessions began, I was in my element. Creating and delivering Magical Adventures for him was the highlight to my week. His Mum cried in the same way I had and I knew that the Purple Magic was working. The impact that my sessions had on this family and the subsequent referrals that I've had from their recommendations make me know that this is the right business for me. From here the snowball effect hit me when I wasn't even looking and I naturally built up more classes, one-to-ones all on Zoom. By the end of July, I'd already made half my initial outlay back! I knew that the gamble was worth it and it was paying off financially, but for me more importantly mentally and emotionally.

My mental health has improved so much since becoming a Relax Kids coach. The Stretch and Breathing techniques are a part of my daily life now. I go to Yoga classes and have begun to meditate. I had lived in such a negative state of mind for so long and suddenly I was representing a company that made work fun and made me feel mentally and physically healthier and happier. The Purple Magic is seriously infectious. My daughter is the same, she uses her breathing unprompted and although she is still scarred from the trauma and we still have massive strides to take, I can't even begin to imagine how much worse she would be if I hadn't been recommended Relax Kids. There is also no rivalry between coaches and the support that I have had from our original Relax Kids coach has been wonderful alongside the Purple Army of other coaches up and down the country. It is an honour to represent them. I would encourage anyone interested to join.

Over the Summer I was running four classes a week and I am now embarking onto my new term-time schedule. It will be different as the children are (finally) back at school, but my target is to take Relax Kids to as many children as possible in my local area via schools, nurseries and continued Zoom sessions. Relax Kids offers targeted sessions to children ages 3-13. My first pre-school Little Stars session is booked and I can't wait to begin to work with pre-schoolers. Chill Skills is planned for pre-bedtime relaxations for age 8-13 year olds along with more Magical Adventures for 5-8-year olds. Not forgetting the all-important Mums who will be joining me to Just Relax. All of these sessions are available on Zoom and so even a second lockdown can't stop me!

As an overall business Blooming Daffodils is about helping parents and their children to build time for self-care into their lives. Mental Health has to be a priority and having battled for many years, I know that I can help to part the black fog and in children to help them to learn how to self-regulate. My slogan is #RELAXTHRIVELEARN and that's exactly it. By learning how to relax, children can thrive at home, at school and can learn to look after themselves mentally as well as physically. I am truly blooming now. From a horrific experience something wonderful has happened. I am now part time at school and will be continuing to build my Relax Kids business around being a mummy. I can't wait to spread the Purple Magic far and wide and to bring little lights into lots of children's lives.

The trauma has changed me but I will not let it define me.

I am strong. I am confident. I am happy.

"Women are the largest untapped reservoir of talent in the world."

HILARY CLINTON

Chapter 15

Signed, Sealed, Delivered

Sally Ashkenazi

Sally is a Notary Public based in South Liverpool. She also sees clients in South and Central Manchester, London and Cumbria but can travel to other areas on request.

Experienced, efficient and personable, Sally is known for putting clients at ease with her plain English, straight talking approach to ensure that her clients understand their legal transactions and implications.

Linkedin: Sally Ashkenazi
Facebook: @mynotarypublic

Website: www.mynotarypublic.co.uk

I am Sally; I am a Notary Public which is a lawyer who specialises in aspects of private international law. Most of my work involves assisting people and businesses who wish to deal with their overseas affairs without leaving the country. I mainly work in Liverpool, Manchester and London and am the director and owner of www.mynotarypublic.co.uk.

I became a lawyer by chance rather than by plan. I studied law at university because I didn't know what I wanted to do and it was a sensible and respected degree that would keep my options open. During my final year, the Dean of my law school persuaded me to go to bar school. I was called to the bar and started working in-house for a London NHS teaching hospital as a junior lawyer in a well appointed legal department.

After a few years, I moved to another hospital as the senior lawyer in a smaller but more challenging department. When I started, the team were at a low point and operating inefficiently. I had the chance to fix things and determine how things should be done. This was a real opportunity to showcase myself and was a huge confidence boost.

It was an exciting time for me. I never knew what challenges the day would bring, and I loved it. I was in my twenties, with good friends, an active social life, a cool job, and confidence.

I decided to leave my London based in-house job as life was calling me to the North-West. By this point I had cross-qualified as a solicitor and took a job with a very good firm of solicitors in Liverpool City Centre.

It felt like a great opportunity. I was working in a well regarded department dealing with high value claims. The clients demanded top level scrutiny so I worked within a team and my decisions were signed off by a partner. It was very different from what I was used to. I still enjoyed the work but was reliant on others to hit deadlines and had to factor in time to explain my reasoning or work flow before things were signed off.

I was no longer accountable, and as time progressed I got used to having that safety net. I was losing my edge and becoming de-skilled.

I stuck with it. I worked long hours but the work certainly had its moments and I worked with some lovely people so there was no incentive to move unless something truly better came along.

When I had children the balance needed to shift. My husband's job does not lend itself to downing tools at 5pm so nursery pickups fell to me. My request to go part time resulted in a four day week and my "day off" was crazy. My eldest daughter was not hitting her developmental milestones so that day was filled with therapy and appointments as well as all the usual mummy stuff and catching up on work. It was hard.

Do we live to work or do we work to live? No matter how we dress it up many of us work to live. Work is a means of feeding our families and financing our activities. At this point, work was doing those things but was encroaching upon other parts of my life. It would creep into evenings and weekends, which really should have been my time. This was never what I wanted but I had no exit strategy.

I had neither the time nor energy to push myself for internal progression. Work expected my gratitude for being permitted to work a four day week. To progress and "prove myself" I would have had to put in even more time. My time. My family time. It was too high a price, and for a prize that didn't really excite me.

Once again I started looking out for other opportunities but I was fussy. I wanted something properly part time, no long commute, and something interesting. A big ask.

Around this time, my husband had the opportunity to take a temporary placement abroad. It had been something we had spoken about and the plan was for me to stay here with the children and we would see each other every few months. There were various reasons for this decision but a couple of months before the trip we made the snap decision to go as a family. I quit my job and packed our bags.

During the visa process my husband had to get his papers notarised before a Notary Public. He asked a few questions about his job and relayed this back to me. Up until this point I didn't really know what a Notary Public was but after that I started looking into it.

The additional training would take a minimum of two and a half years and by the time we decided that I would join my husband abroad I had enrolled for the first study module.

I ended up completing that and a further module remotely. I worked through the online study materials and viewed videos of the seminars and workshops and sat my first two exams overseas before returning to the UK for the final one and a half years of the course. I sat my third exam two days after my youngest daughter was born and qualified when she was one.

Whilst I was studying I was able to be a nearly full time mum to my girls. They went to nursery one day a week and the rest of the time they were with me. It was hard at times as we had no family support and my husband was working crazy hours, but it was fun. I really got to know my girls and take the time with them. Our schedule was led by them and I could manage our time for our convenience and enjoyment. It was great and I wanted that to continue when I started working so I thought long and hard about how I could run my business whilst still being meaningfully present for my children.

Before I set up www.mynotarypublic.co.uk and my notary public service I stripped away the traditional image of how a legal practice should look and considered what clients want and need. I thought about how I could achieve this whilst also remaining a present and mindful parent to my children. At a basic level clients want their work done to a good level by someone competent. Many clients also prefer to see someone who can see them at a convenient time, quickly and efficiently and who can make a complicated process seem simple.

I sometimes see clients in the evenings or at weekends and also offer popular express appointments for certain types of work. During the Covid-19 lockdown I operated as a drive through service. This is not what you would expect from a legal practice but it worked.

My NHS experience has served me well. Working in an organisation of non-lawyers taught me to discuss legal concepts in plain English without dumbing it down or overcomplicating. I think this is what clients want. They want a job done properly and they need to understand the legal process with which they are engaged. Communication is key.

My girls will always be my biggest priority. I do the school run and ferry them to their various activities, make their meals, listen to them read, chat to them, play with them and help them learn. They get to see me, and they get to see my work and sometimes even help out by stamping envelopes. I really hope it motivates them to see that there will come a point in their life when they can write their own rules. At the moment, as far as they are concerned any job which requires a multitude of stamps, stickers, ribbon and an impressive embossing press must be worth studying for.

"I wake up every morning and think to myself "How far can I push the company in the next 24 hours"

———

LEAH BUSQUE

Chapter 16

More than meets the eye

Lisa Betsworth

If someone had told Lisa five years ago what the next five years would look like I think she would have locked herself away.

But here she is, still standing and her recruitment business is going from strength to strength.

Facebook: @SliceRecruitment
Linkedin: Lisabetsworth

I was born in 1981 in Munster, West Germany. My dad was a serving soldier in the British Army. I lived with my parents and elder sister. We moved around Germany mostly however we also did two years in Hong Kong which was an amazing experience. Due to this I attended various schools until the age of nine. One Christmas I remember going to the airport with my dad to take my sister to catch her flight back to university in the UK and I saw loads of kids in school uniform. I realised they were all army kids flying back to the UK to go to boarding school. At that point I thought, I think I fancy some of that. In my head boarding school was like the orphanage in Annie, I watched that a lot as a kid, but these kids didn't look a thing like Annie and they were not singing "It's a hard knock life". So, the search began for a school.

I started at Ranby House in Nottinghamshire. My parents will tell the story of how when we visited the schools my behaviour at Ranby was impeccable. I was the model child, however the other school, not so much. Apparently even at nine years of age when I saw something I wanted, I went for it. Ranby gave me the ability to mix with various people from all walks of life and this was the start of my independence. Six years of flying solo back and forth to Germany where my parents still lived forced me to grow up, but I loved my school days.

I finished my schooling in boarding school and went to a sixth form college from where I applied for University places. I was accepted into several Uni's to do Leisure and Tourism Management but felt it was not right for me so declined the placement and decided to go and study hair and beauty.

I sort of fell into recruitment a few years after that. I went to register at an agency my friend worked at and while she was on the phone I got chatting to the lovely lady on reception, only she wasn't the receptionist, unbeknown to me, she was the MD. She called me into her office and asked me if I had ever considered a career in Recruitment. Well the rest as they say is history.

I loved my job, but as it was an independent agency, there wasn't much in the way of progression. I could have stayed there forever and probably made some really good money but I was young and fiercely ambitious and I wanted to go somewhere where I could move up the ladder and fast. This forced me to move over to work for nationals.

I had a great time working for some of the corporate big boys over many years and found myself working on some great projects with companies such as RSPCA, Carphone Warehouse and Clarins. I worked my way up with various companies to management level always moving to a better job and working up the ladder but still in recruitment.

At this time, I was happy at work and was also happy in my private life and was planning to marry. Two days before the wedding catastrophe struck and I was made redundant!!!

By this point my parents lived in Spain and my new husband and I were not going on honeymoon for a few month after the wedding so we decided to head to Spain for a few days following the wedding to have some down time. It was there at about 2am one morning I sat bolt upright in bed and shouted "I'm going to do this on my own", God knows what my husband must have thought.

Like most people who set up a business out of some sort of crisis rather than plan, it soon became apparent that I was better off working for myself and so I started my own company and after a lot of deliberating I named it Tiro. Tiro is what the new recruits into the Trojan army were called, I thought that was really clever!

This company ticked along nicely at first and I took on another person so that I could do the strategic work and they could do the resourcing and day to day work. I also invested in office space so that I was actually going to work and not working from home

The company had its ups and downs and at the time I found out I was pregnant!! That was not in the business plan I can tell you, but we made it work. I was e-mailing clients as they wheeled me down for my C Section and within forty-eight hours of having my beautiful baby girl the laptop was never too far away. I gave up the office space and had my own office built in my back garden. I still had an employee and together we plodded on.

My daughter was two years old and, in an attempt to lose the baby weight I signed up to do a personal challenge like no other. Shine Bright Like a Diamond was a ten-week challenge for women that made you focus on fitness, nutrition and mindset. The ten weeks culminated in a grand finale with a show and a dinner. The Diamonds, as we were called were the entertainment, showing off our body transformations in both evening ware and underwear, so if ever you felt like having the slice of pizza or that bar of chocolate, the thought of being on a stage in front of two hundred plus people in very little soon made you change your mind. I trained harder than I had ever trained in my life, hitting the gym five times a week. I was struggling with my hip towards the end but got through it with the help of some exceptionally good friends. After the show the pain never went away so to appease these friends and my family, I decided to go to the doctors thinking that I had probably trapped a nerve whilst exercising.

The GP was in the same frame of mind as me and thought a bit of physio would sort it. As a belt and braces job she sent me for x-rays and told to come back for the results in ten days' time. However, I was telephoned two days later and asked to come in to the surgery where the bomb shell was dropped and I was told I had cancer!!!!

I did not know what to do but I just had to get through this, for my daughter if nothing else. I had an incredibly good friend working for me at the time who kept the business ticking over whilst I went through six months of chemo. I did what I could but because of the circumstances I left most of it to my friend.

After going through the treatment and losing my hair I started to wear wigs and found some extremely helpful charities out there who are willing to help people who had lost their hair through medical reasons. I tried to keep everything as normal as possible for the sake of my little girl. Her birthday, Christmas, they all fell during the six months I was having chemo but I made sure I was the best mum I could be.

The business was struggling and at this time it seemed as if most of the jobs we were bidding for we seemed to be bidding against another independent company. That company was owned by someone I knew and we had done some work together in the past. As soon as he found out I was ill he wanted to help as much as he could.

After a while we decided that it was best if we amalgamated our businesses which we did and unfortunately there was only room for me in this new concept and I had to finish my friend. I felt horrendous, but being the beautiful human that she is she totally understood and in fact encouraged me to do it saying I deserved a shot at less stress. This meant that I now got a wage and no overheads so for me it worked well at the time.

The amalgamation seemed to me to be a success. We were surpassing targets and everyone was saying what a great idea it was. One day he called me in the office and said that he was letting me go! Why? I'm not sure I will ever really understand!! I was gutted!! I was getting over my cancer but had lost my business. I was angry, scared, upset. I had sacrificed everything including my relationship with my best friend and now I had nothing to show for it.

There were some dark days that followed, I didn't know what I wanted to do going forward and I think the events of the previous twelve month finally hit home.

After some time licking my wounds and feeling sorry for myself, I started to work again. I picked up the odd bit of work from some of my very loyal clients who followed me. I refused to admit I was back in business as that required confidence I just didn't have at that point. After five months of doing this it was pointed out to me that like it or not I was in fact back in business and it was going better than Tiro ever did. I started again with Slice.

Today Slice is the business I always wanted. Built on solid service and strong morals. I want to help support SME's in growing their business however I can. I have taken everything that I learnt from Tiro and my training over the years and applied it into Slice. I will forever be grateful for the clients that have stood by me over the years and to my friend who is still my biggest cheerleader today. Slice is growing and little by little changing the perception that all recruiters are nothing more than aggressive salespeople.

Looking back, would I change anything? No, I don't think I would. I'm a firm believer in fate and what is meant for you won't pass you by. My journey, while it has not always been smooth sailing is what makes me who I am today!

"Don't ever let somebody tell you that you can't do something."

VEDIKA GOEL

Chapter 17

It All Turned Out Different

Kirsty Gibbons

Kirsty lives in Exeter, Devon with her young son. Whilst being born and raised there Kirsty has been fortunate enough to explore this great planet. More recently Kirsty has settled back into Devon with her young son. There she enjoys the semi rural life and all it has to offer.

Kirsty now runs K&K Business Consulting with her business partner Kate and also writes for her own blog. In her downtime, when it happens, she loves exploring what the area has to offer and winding down with her arts and crafts projects.

www.kkbservices.com

www.wordsofamum.co.uk

When Jane first asked about contributing to this book, I thought it was a fantastic opportunity. This being for two reasons. Firstly, I have always wanted to be an author. What's that saying "everyone has a book inside them". I think that is certainly true in my case and who knows it might be the stepping stone I need. Secondly, because if I can inspire or help one person through my writing that would be fantastic. Now don't get me wrong this isn't going to be a massively inspiring chapter. It's just a chapter about life and how I ended up where I am today. I can certainly say my sixteen year old self didn't see me ending up where I am today but I guess that is true of almost everyone.

In my childhood and early teens I always thought I would end up a teacher. It's hard to believe how passionate I was about it back then. It didn't even enter my mind that I would do anything else. But talking to family now it makes sense I didn't end up a teacher. A lot of my family always thought I would end up an entrepreneur. I was always planning something, thinking of new ideas and trying to create them. So, it's natural I followed a different path than what I originally thought I would.

By my late teens I have moved on from wanting to be a teacher. I had changed my mind to lawyer and by my early twenties I was studying law. There was one major distraction in my twenties and that was my love of travel. I was certainly hit by a massive sense of wanderlust. Not that I have a problem with that. It's actually one of the reasons that I ended up working hard. It gave me the ability to travel and work abroad. My twenties were definitely about travel and studying. To a certain extent, although hindered somewhat at the moment, I guess it is now. I still have that wanderlust inside me and I want my son to experience the joys and experience travel can bring. Who knows how the new normal will turn out with travel. But I do hope that my son gets to experience how amazing it can be.

In case you were wondering I did complete my studies in law and worked in law. I didn't take the conventional route of jumping from college straight into university. If I am honest, I had no idea what I wanted to do in college. I took an administration course because it seemed like the best bet for someone who had no idea what they wanted to do. I think that is certainly a point to emphasise. Not everyone knows what they want to do straight away and it's okay to change your mind. I never had any pressure from my parents about what I studied. I was free to decide what path I wanted to go down in terms of education and employment. Whether that was studying or going straight into employment. This is something I am extremely thankful for. I never felt I had to do something study wise for someone else. It is one of the reasons I didn't think twice about changing from administration to law. In fact, I am grateful I have experience from both industries it's certainly helped in running our business.

Studying and practising law honestly wasn't how I expected it to turn out. It didn't initially give me that satisfaction of helping people. Initially, and probably naively, I had a picture of something out of an American TV show in my head– cliché I know. I started out in criminal law, moved to family law and eventually ended up in litigation. To my surprise litigation was where I got the biggest sense of achievement. I worked with people who were under represented and unfairly treated and had protected characteristics under the Equality Act. Whilst this was very rewarding it was also very stressful and led to me wanting to take a break. Well it was one of the reasons, I always wanted to travel further than the usual two week holiday would allow.

Now that I look back, I really do see how fortunate I have been in being able to travel. I had seen some beautiful countries and been able to do it without the worry of the new normal. I will never forget the experiences and life challenges it brought me and nor do I want to.

But guess what whilst I was away, I didn't truly get away from law! Whilst in Sydney I worked for a law firm although not for long. It was long enough to top up my bank account for onward travel.

Thinking about it travel wasn't all that plain sailing. There was an infected insect bite, an earthquake and a cyclone. Maybe I am not the best travel partner! But in all honesty despite all this I really do feel like I gained a lot from travelling. I have so many fond memories of my travels and can often be found going through old photographs. I have boxes and boxes of photographs from those travels and looking through them brings a smile to my face. Not only are there fond memories it also taught me a lot. I am less materialistic, calmer and so much better at being organised. It also refocussed my mind on my love of writing. Perhaps there is a book there too!

Anyway, I digressed there a little didn't I? After getting back from travelling you guessed it, I ended up back in law. You see law is a strange area and it draws you back in. It's something you work very hard at and can, in the right situation, give you both enjoyment and satisfaction. But at the same time doing well in law can often lead to your personal life suffering. The deadlines very often can't be moved and as a result I would often work on my days off. Don't get me wrong law is right for some people but full time it isn't right for me.

I worked in law again for a good number of years before something happened in my personal life. My natural reaction to this, and the pressures of work, led me to jump ship once again and I ended up in America. I went on to spend two years in America, Texas to be precise, but it didn't fulfil my sense of wanderlust like Australia, New Zealand and all the other countries did. Looking back running from what happened in my personal life wasn't necessarily the best decision. However, at the same time it led to the birth of my son. Now that doesn't mean my son was a mistake. He absolutely was not and looking at him now whilst I write it definitely isn't the case. He's a happy cheeky two year old with character. He knows his own mind (wonder where he gets that from!) but he is also very polite and a little too clever at times.

Whilst the birth of my son caught me off guard a little. Without a doubt there have been times where I thought what am I doing? This doesn't make me or anyone else a bad parent. It makes you completely normal and I can honestly say I don't think anyone is truly ready to be a parent. This is a very important message I want to put out there. It's not okay to make someone feel inadequate when the reality is, they are probably doing pretty well. There have been times where I have dropped my son off at nursery and forgotten to brush my hair. It was only when I saw some of the immaculately turned out women that I realised this. At first it used to get to me but not now. I've learned to take a step back and appreciate what I have. I have a healthy and happy son who hasn't wanted for much. I am also running my own business and on the property ladder – I think I am doing okay!

Where I am today wasn't all plain sailing. Like I said when I was pregnant, I wasn't prepared and I didn't really know where to start. At one point I also found myself homeless although I wasn't living on the street. I ended up moving back in with mum and dad and whilst this wasn't the ideal situation it was a stepping stone. As soon as I moved in, whilst pregnant, I think I worked the hardest I ever have. This came from a mixture of a broken heart and nesting. Thankfully I had been working remotely for a number of clients before this all happened and I stepped up my game. I joined forces with my friend, and now business partner, Kate and together we started up K&K Business Consulting. Our experience in both law and administration has helped no end in setting up business. It's also skills we now use to help clients. K&K Business Consulting gives me that balance that law alone never gave me. So, whilst some might feel it's a wasted career it is certainly not how I feel. I am happy with the job that I do and contrary to what some might say working with a friend works for us. We bounce off each other, offer a different perspective, are a sounding board for each other and we achieve.

As you can imagine setting up a business takes a lot of work and a lot of effort. In the beginning I decided to take on a part time job to supplement my income. I wanted something regular that I could rely on and doing this worked perfectly. Thankfully the job was flexible and it allowed me to work around my business and my son. Don't get me wrong it was hard work and there were days, like any other business owner, that I wanted to scream and give up. Thankfully I didn't as I can honestly say running K&K Business Consulting has been amazing. We have some fantastic clients and we truly are passionate about their businesses. I no longer have that day job and focus all my time on the business, my son and my relationship. Whilst these last few months have been testing, down to the pandemic, we are moving on. Helping clients adapt, work remotely and supporting them in making their businesses great. We really do love doing this and seeing clients grow is amazing.

In terms of my personal life I have mended that broken heart, bought a property in my name and met someone new. Here and now I am positive about the outlook and proud of what I have achieved. I won't bore you with all the details of my personal life I'll save that for another book!

If my story, although very condensed for this chapter, helps other people that would be amazing. Even if it's just the smallest reassurance I am okay with that. If not, I hope it's been a relatively interesting read.

Lastly, I cannot sign off without talking about the people that are around me now. They have been truly amazing. I know I am very fortunate to have that. I won't bore you with naming everyone but if you are in my life now you are one of those people.

"Trying to do it all and expecting it all can be done exactly right is a recipe for disappointment. Perfection is the enemy."

SHERYL SANDBERG

Chapter 18

The Girl from the Dingle

Author Natalie Reeves Billing

Natalie Reeves Billing is a Liverpool lass with a spooky sense of humour. She loves to write fantastical stories for young audiences, and dabbles in poetry. Natalie spent most of her early career in the music industry as a performer and songwriter. This inevitably lead to storytelling.

Natalie is a fellow of the School of Social Entrepreneurs and a student of The Golden Egg Academy. She is mentored under the Lloyds Bank SSE program. She is published in several anthologies with her poetry and short stories, including Writing on the Wall and 8N Publishing USA, with its Winter Chills collection. She is currently delivering creative workshops throughout Merseyside. Natalie's children's books, My Mummy is a Monster and My Daddy is a Monster (the Monstrous Me collection) and Ben and the Bug, a story through the eyes of a germ, are winners of The Best Children's Book category, Gold and Silver in the Mum's Choice awards 2020 and out on Amazon via www.lolliplodge.net/store.

Split Perspectivz Ltd

Website: www.nataliebillingreeves.com
Twitter: @BillingReeves
Facebook: @NatalieRBillingAuthor
Instagram: @natalie_reeves_billing

The story of me begins in a terraced house in Toxteth. Mum left London— gave up the high life, squatting and dating the east end's weirdest punk rockers—and came home carrying a bit more than a backpack. In years to come, I would be reminded of the offers she'd turned down in order to provide for me. She'd probably cried throwing away her skin-tight bondage pants.

We lived in a two-bedroom house in the Holyland, a name given to four fairly ordinary streets with biblical names. Mum and I shared a bed in the creepiest, coldest room imaginable. Mum's collection of porcelain dolls loomed down at us from every conceivable angle, most of them clowns and jesters. None you'd want to see after 7pm.

Times were tough, but the memories still fill me with an innocent joy I can't quite regain. Like at Christmas. Uncle Billy would knock on our door late on the eve, delivering toys he'd hidden from my prying eyes. George from the fruit shop brought tangerines, all wrapped up in their own papers, sitting in little cardboard molds. The multi-coloured tree lights twinkling in our front parlour. No one was allowed in there. It was saved for a special occasion that never came. Our tree was off-limits to all but those passing by on the frigid streets outside.

Every weekend we'd come together for Sunday Roast, our plates loaded with teetering gravy towers. Aunty Doris would get the biggest plate if you could call it that. Most country folk would call it a trough. We would balance our bottoms wherever we could find a ledge, for the dining table was in the room we weren't permitted in. We'd eat on our knees while the TV blared. It gave us material to argue over. The meal would finish perfectly with a cup of milky, sugary tea. The type nans make for their grandkids when they're first setting out on their great English tea romance.

Everything about my life made sense then. It was bliss. I adored the safety of my family. We lived so close together you could open your front window and yell, and the whole clan would gather in a few seconds flat. Primary school was a great. I was this massive child with a flat nose, broken in a skirmish with the art room table. That, and an unfortunate hairdo that looked something like a stegosaurus's spine, meant I was given the rather unflattering name of 'Nasty Pasty.' It served me well because no one except Hannah Standish messed with me, and that was fine because she ate her scabs. Hardcore.

Even then, I had a love affair with writing. Mum stoked my creative passions editing my poems, and in some cases, writing the entire thing. Little did Radio Merseyside know that the Primary school's Carol Competition winner of 1992 was actually a thirty-year-old woman.

I met my best friend in secondary school. Two years of heaven, we had together. The kind of friendship you can never replicate. We were two impoverished youngsters in a reasonably rich school. Threadbare Jonathon Aston tights and reeking of Dewberries. We wanted to be famous, so we started fundraising and practiced our harmonies on the 27 bus, the strangest route in the universe. David Attenborough would have had a field day observing some of the specimens we met. Sometimes we made a fair bit of cash; other times, we just got our heads kicked in. But nothing could stand in our way. We called ourselves 'Me and Her' but when another friend joined, it became, 'Me, Her and Someone Else' and that wasn't good. No one takes you seriously with a name like that, but our harmonies were first rate. Everyone at the 'Working Man's Buffalo Club' in Tuebrook, said so.

But when my boobs started growing, and I discovered boys, that friendship faded. She belonged on the back of Prince Charming's horse, I belonged in a gingerbread house, stirring potions. I always favoured the darkness. I had no real role models of what a man should be. My grandad was quiet and respectful, but often distant, and I knew nothing of my dad other than he wore an enviable blonde Mohican and often put his fist through car windows.

My strange dynamic with men continued through most of my twenties. I was intrigued by them, but when in relationships, I became unhinged. I found their love a weakness. When boys were too nice, I started with the games, picking at them bit by bit. Unravelling and stripping them down until there was nothing left but resentment.

I left school at sixteen and did my A-Levels at college, but it was music and creative arts that I really wanted to do. I enrolled at the community college. That was where I picked up the members of my band. There was a floppy-haired guy with an uneven tan who watched me wherever I went. Who'd have guessed that he would be my co-writer in a signed band and travelling the globe in just two short years?

We moved in together. The creative connection was almost supernatural. I wouldn't have to say a thing, and the right chord would accompany me: the right rhythm, speed, and harmony. We held auditions, recruited some cool people, and became a family. Five young Scousers with not a pot to piddle in, but with aspirations way beyond what society would typically allow such a motley crew.

The recording contract hadn't been with us a week before we were sat on a plane to LA at the beginning of a new, popstar life. The weeks passed in a giddy fog, as we entertained the idea that we may actually have made it. With limousines ferrying us around, and luxury suites laid on at the Ritz, it certainly seemed to be the case. We rubbed shoulders with people we recognised but had never met. Our music was being produced by men who, only days before, had got wasted with the Red Hot Chilli Peppers. With Mike Tyson appearing in our music videos and appointments with surgeons for certain body enlargements, who'd have thought that it would all come crashing down? That the man we worshipped, our record boss, the Music Mogul with the Midas touch, Dr. Henry Jones, would be given a prison sentence no mortal man could survive.

And so, the government shut him down for fraud, locked him away in the desert, and bargain-binned our albums, and I went home with my tail between my legs and a heart of solid lead. Discontentment grew in the sadness of our band. The very sight of each other reminded us of all we'd lost. So young and with egos the size of the moon, we felt a huge sense of failure and shame. Who would believe us? The lives we'd lived—the things we'd done. We'd be just another disillusioned drunkard with a story. So, we brushed it under the carpet, disbanded, and never talked of it again. To us, it didn't exist.

I had a brief flirtation with a solo career, but it was done. Music was too painful now. My relationship ended, and I moved into the city centre, dreaming of doing something completely different, as far removed from music as I could possibly get.

Recycling!

A friend was doing quite well in electronic processing. I had a small pot of money I was yet to squander. It made sense to invest, and so I became someone else for a few years—a sensible person…ish. I had entrepreneurial hobbies that took me on trips to Brazil and the rainforest, Argentina, and Morocco. Still, it was a strange life, as lives are when you aren't being your authentic self. I was a business-bot, programmed to succeed in an arena I didn't give two flying ones about. An industry that couldn't break my heart, because I didn't care enough about it.

But, the old need to create never truly left me. I never could do anything by the book. My recycling yard piloted a Rag and Bone Van scheme. A legion of workers dressed in flat caps and cravats travelling around the mean streets of Old Swan in a converted Ice Cream van. Playing, 'Any old iron' over a tannoy. God bless those poor boys. These were not my proudest days, more Del Boy than Beyonce. But it taught me one thing. You can't hide from yourself. Your body will act out. Find other, stranger opportunities to create its art. There we dark days here as I battled the demons. We will pass through without loitering. Sometimes, when we stare into the abyss, the abyss stares back.

But then, I met my polar opposite. Never have two people been so different. Our first date included a full tutorial on how to keep clover out your front lawn. I fell in love with him right there. This was a guy with no front whatsoever, and I was so over the big talkers. If I was ever going to do this family thing, it had to be with someone who knew good grass when he saw it. And that it wasn't it greener on the other side.

I didn't think children would factor into my future but thank God they did, because I was born again when I became a mum. After an initial adjustment period, when I finally laid to rest that selfish, egotistical diva I once was, I discovered ME. Words and stories came back, but this time as bedtime tales for my precious angels.

And it finally sunk in. Writing had been my one constant through it all. Expressing myself through imagery and analogy. I was a writer, and as it turns out, a bloody good one. I had never been kind to ME before or allowed myself a compliment, but now I'm proud of the woman I've become. Despite everything I've said here, and many million things I haven't, I am finally living the life I was meant to live.

I am a person who has overcome depression, disappointment, poverty, and abuse. A person who has lied, cheated, and hurt others. But, I am also a person who has learned the harsh lessons life has thrown my way. I have loved, cherished, laughed, supported, encouraged, and helped, and those are the things I am taking forward with me.

When the pandemic hit, I'd just started a new social enterprise called Split Perspectivz. Helping schools and community centres in underfunded areas to access quality reading materials and literacy aids. I launched my first two children's books in May, and they went to number one in their categories. I have found a way to fulfill my career goals while also raising a family and helping others, and that is the most sacred balance I could ever achieve.

"Destiny is name often given in retrospect to choices that had dramatic consequences"

JK ROWLING

Chapter 19

"This Is Me"

Fiona Wallace

Founder of This Is Me and Network Leader for MIB International Women Empowerment Network. Fiona's passion is empowering women to feel more confident, have glowing natural bare skin, reduce breakouts, have a healthy gut and love their body inside and out through the power of Aloe.

This year has been such a roller-coaster for her with her postnatal depression and she wants to empower and support women. Through sharing her story whilst providing a safe space for women to talk and to share her passion for natural products.

In August 2020 she became a Network Leader for MIB International Women Empowerment Network the whole ethos of MIB International aligns so much with her and it has been an amazing journey so far. She loves the online community of like-minded women all working together no one needs to struggle alone they are here to support you in your business.

Instagram: @mamashustleandbustle
Facebook group: This is me - Supportive Online Cafe
Facebook Group: MIB Int Networking Aberdeen

In November 2015 I was planning my wedding in Rhodes, Greece. I worked full time as a Student Finance Manager at a University and had done for fifteen years. I loved my job, but I needed an extra income to pay for my wedding. I didn't have time for another job as my daughter was three years old and I had sixty-mile round trip commute to work. I started to look for something that I could do from home around all my other commitments. I came across a post on Facebook and it looked ideal no monthly commitment, no monthly cost, no stock to hold, work as and when you wanted. I thought this is too good to be true I had never heard of MLM or network marketing before. I replied to the post and was sent over some information I took one look and it ticked all the boxes.

I couldn't wait to get started and I got registered straight away with Forever – The Aloe Vera Company I loved the idea of being in business for myself but without any overheads, no huge start us cost, help and support of a long-standing global business and an amazing business mentor. Was I nervous yes, I had never sold anything before, and I didn't know anything about plant-based products or skincare?

Something that really stood out to me was the company's values and ethics. It is a family run company and the help and support given to normal people just like me was so reassuring. The support and training along the way has been second to none and I have seen a lot of training in my career in Higher Education. I also really liked the fact that everything came with a sixty-day money back guarantee now you don't see that very often.

We got married in Rhodes at Kalithea Springs in May 2016. We even had a champagne boat trip to take us from the ceremony in Kalithea to our Taverna for our reception. It was like a fairy tale. I'm so proud that I was able to pay for it all and take twenty-one of our family with us.

After our wedding I decided to continue my business as it fitted in and around everything else that I had going on and the extra income was great it paid for our two holidays each year.

In 2019 I was pregnant with my second daughter I had the most horrendous pregnancy with sickness and pelvic girdle pain. By the end of it I could hardly walk, and the pain was really starting to get to me. After having Eden, it went away and then I got the baby blues or that's what I thought it was. In March 2020 when Eden was seven months old, I found out that I had postnatal depression this was just two weeks before lockdown. I was so emotional, irritable, feeling low and I couldn't do much. It was like my bum was stuck to the seat, going anywhere gave me huge anxiety even just shopping.It was like having a big black cloud following me about. I couldn't remember anything. I had brain fog constantly and I was always tired and couldn't get to sleep for my brain thinking all the time.

I hid all this behind a smile and tried to pretend I was okay I would also avoid any social interaction I didn't even want to answer the phone or message anyone. I had lost all interest in my appearance and didn't want to even get dressed.

I went to the doctors to see if they could help me, having someone to talk to and knowing that I wasn't going crazy was such a relief. Then lockdown happened my husband was still working full time and I was at home with my two girls Zarah who was eight years old and Eden was seven months. I was trying to home school, run my business all with a baby hanging off my leg so we gave up on the home school and just enjoyed our extra time together.

I am grateful for lockdown as it gave me time to reflect and re-evaluate. We all get so busy being busy we never stop and take time to reflect. The slower pace of life with no rushing and no going out the house gave me time. I loved the slower pace of life and I started to feel more like myself. Looking after your mental health is so important but we always seem to put ourselves last on the priority list. Lockdown gave me time and I started taking care of me be that a cuppa in peace, a bath, watching Netflix or a face mask now I had never been in to face masks before lockdown. I wish I had tried them years ago it's so nice to stop relax and pop a mask on. I also started to do a gratitude journal which has really helped me to stay positive and focus on what is good rather than the bad.

My self care includes a sleep meditation to help my brain to switch off its just twenty minutes long and I never hear the end of it. Every weekend self care is scheduled in. Zarah and I have movie night and a face mask. You need to have time off and when you do have time off switch off your phone and be present you will never have today again so make it count.

With my hormones being all over the place and me not looking after myself my skin was a mess this really knocked my confidence. I had breakouts all the time, big dark puffy circles around my eyes, patchy skin those baby wipes were doing nothing for me.

I had all the products and no motivation to use them previously I always thought I was too busy. How wrong was I. I now have a daily skincare routine morning and night, no hassle no faff its quick and simple what a difference. Instantly I seen my skin improve and over about thirty days my skin was glowing. I can't believe how easy it actually is and that I didn't start years ago it has taken me until I'm thirty-eight to start to look after my skin. When I say simple it really is I just use my Hydrating Cleanser in the shower in the morning, then a little firming serum to sort out the smile lines, then my magic eye cream and finally my restoring cream to make sure my skin has the hydration it needs. It takes less that a few mins morning and night.

Lockdown has helped me get really clear on what I'm passionate about I have never been clearer on where I'm going and what I want to do.

My passion is empowering women to feel more confident, have glowing natural bare skin, reduce the breakouts, have a healthy gut and love their body from the inside and out. Not only by using my Aloe-based skincare products but also by drinking the world's only pure aloe vera drinking gel.
I'm often greeted by surprise when I tell them that I drink aloe every day and so do my whole family. Eden gets so excited in the morning screaming at the fridge to get her peach aloe! Who doesn't want to have glowing skin, strong nails, a great digestive system, a strong immune system, good healthy joints and a healthy balanced gut? A healthy gut equals a healthy mind, body and soul.

No one needs to feel self-conscious about their skin or hide under make up.

Your skin is your largest organ in your body and it's the last organ to get any nutrition either from food you eat or supplements. We need to help it from inside and out.

Lockdown definitely saved me it gave me clarity around what is important, It gave me confidence and It gave me, me back.

I have never felt better about myself I am full of energy, less bloated and my skin is glowing if you look back at photos on my social media you can see the difference no more dark circles, the redness has reduced and even my frown or smile lines are less prominent.

I never recommend any skincare to my clients without doing a free evaluation first as it must be personal to you it's not a one size fits all.

I am working hard this year to grow my business and to reach more women. I have never been clearer on my vision and my mission to empower women to take control be that to work from home flexibly or to empower them to feel more confident and love their body from the inside out.

I am on a complete mission and nothing is going to stop me the joy and pleasure I get from all the amazing feedback from my team and testimonials from my clients is second to none. It fills me with pride that I can help and empower women all around the world.

With my newfound purpose in August 2020 I found MIB International Women Empowerment Network I was completely inspired by Leona Burton and Heather Rose. I became the Network Leader for Aberdeen and Aberdeenshire. This has enabled me to support and empower women in my local area through networking and training at an affordable price making it accessible for all. To think when I started my business I was terrified of live videos and now I'm regularly live in groups and on my profile. The support and belief in me from other women in business has really helped with my self-confidence.

I am by no means at the end of my journey as just at the end of September I had slipped back down in to that hole of doom my big black cloud was back I wasn't feeling great my emotions were all over the place and what I found is that through sharing the ups and the downs along the way I can help women to realise they are not alone. We all have ups and downs and the messages of support that I get from my new online friends has been amazing.

Many women have reached out to me and opened up about their problems that they have never felt able to tell anyone else and through this I decided to set up This is Me – Supportive Online Café which is a safe Facebook group where I want to help women by providing support, motivation, a safe place to rant about a crappy day and to share health and skincare tips along the way. This has been so rewarding and much needed in the current circumstances of us all being stuck at home and not having our normal community around us for support.

My top tip would be feel the fear and do it anyway. I had always refused point blank to do live videos. I was worried about what people would think, what would I say, what if I mess it up. In August 2020 I bit the bullet with a lot of encouragement from a fellow amazing woman in business and pushed that go live button. Now I wish I had started sooner as the world is not going to end when you push the go live button on Facebook. If you mess up, then own it as you know what we are all human and we all make mistakes its how we deal with them that matters.

My second top tip would be to network get out there and surround yourself with like minded women. I started networking in August this year and already it has had a huge impact on my business and me personally. It has grown my confidence and opened my business to a whole host of people that I would never have met or crossed paths with if I hadn't been networking.

"If people are doubting how far you can go, go so far that you can't hear them anymore."

———

MICHELE RUIZ

Chapter 20

The Stay At Home Mum

Liz Johnson

Early Years Teacher come stay at home Wife and Mum!

Liz, at the time of going to print, is a 35 year old Mum of a two and a half year old and a seven month old. She tries to inspire, build up and encourage women (and men) to live their best lives, through positivity, words of wisdom, moral support, love and understanding.

Facebook: @thestayathomemum
Instagram: @mrslizjohnson17 @lizjohnsonthestayathomemum

What defines success and to be successful? The Oxford dictionary determines success to be "(uncountable) the fact that you have achieved something that you want and have been trying to do or get." So it is society itself that has blurred that definition to mean success to be rich or famous, high powered in your job or society, to have many assets... or instagram followers.

To be perfectly honest when I was asked to write for this book I wondered why on earth my little life mattered. How could I help or inspire other women, successful women, or women who wanted to become successful in whatever they do. I barely have my life together and I certainly wouldn't think I had anything to offer any other women. But I have learned that, sometimes, you just have to go with it and believe in what someone else sees in you. Obviously there are caveats; I'm not saying believe everything everyone says as you will be in for a whole lot of hurt if you do that. But, in those circumstances where people see in you strength, success, inspiration and encouragement, then don't argue. Embrace it!

By 'trade' I am an Early Years Teacher. I completed my post graduate EYTS in 2015 and was a Deputy Nursery Manager at a lovely nursery in West Bridgford, Nottingham. I met my husband the year we both turned thirty and ended up moving to Chesterfield as he, and his parents, run a successful business here. I struggled to find somewhere here that fit in with my teaching ethos and between that and my mental health struggles I gave up work. I love working with children and it was hard to make that decision. However, I know my beliefs on childcare and the ways in which they should learn and nothing was sitting right with me. I was fortunate to be able to give up work as many people are not in that position.

Fast forward a few years from meeting my husband and I am a stay at home wife and mum to two beautiful children. Our daughter, our second born, was born on Mother's Day, March 22nd 2020, the day before we were put into lockdown. I am adamant my husband's actions are the reason my waters broke; a six am trip to Morrisons for when it opened and he managed to buy toilet roll and pasta. He sent me over the edge!

Having a baby in lockdown is so surreal and I am glad it wasn't my first experience of becoming a mother. Strangely, I didn't have any mental health issues this time despite a worldwide pandemic and UK lockdown but it wasn't easy all the same. When you become a parent you question yourself, who you are, are you still you, and you mourn the loss of your old self in some ways. I've read a few things on this and opinions are mixed as to whether these feelings are ok, but do you know what? They completely are. For my husband and I, we were fortunate to fall pregnant again and I lost my identity once again.

Keeping hold of some form of my identity and learning through these months of obscurity is one of my greater successes. I am actually a much stronger person now than I have ever been. Every season and transition in your life calls for re-evaluation of who you are, who you want to be, why you want to achieve something and who you are achieving it for. As a young girl all I ever wanted to be was a wife and mum (that was after I gave up on mermaid and lollipop lady!) My mum was a great example to me and she was the very definition of success.

No one can ever truly prepare you for anything in life but for me my first dip into motherhood was a time of intense pressure and great scrutiny. The emotions, the sleep deprivation, the not knowing what's right or wrong leads onto greater questions, can I do this? Who have I become? Am I even me? I'm quite an open person and I don't generally hold back on questioning things. Having had post natal depression with my son and pre natal depression with my Daughter I have journeyed further into my brain than ever before and realised that no, I'm not the same person. I am still me, but I have evolved into a new definition of me. Before my children I was me but with less responsibilities. I could jump in the car and drive to Spain if I wanted. I still could now, it would just take me two days, ten suitcases and a Tetris theme tune to pack the car to! What I think I am saying is in your journey to succeed you must constantly re evaluate where you are in your current season and who you are in this season. You may need to adjust and to change just as the seasons change but the essence of you remains the same.

I've thought quite a lot about this chapter about me; someone who can empower other women to become a Lioness and I have come to the realisation that my success won't look anything like your success, therefore we shouldn't be striving to be 'as successful as Joe Bloggs'. Although I reckon Joe Bloggs could have earned a penny or two by now if he had trademarked his name!

I consider myself to have achieved a few big successes in life so far, and have had many 'failings' for want of a better term. I said 'big' successes as I think success can be differentiated even within the terms of our own success. We can have daily and weekly goals that we can be successful in, as well as more long term goals we are striving for.

In the long term though we tend to look back over our lives and remember the big ones; for me that was my first class honours degree in Psychology. I returned to education as a mature student to compete my A levels and get a degree - Success. Another one would be gaining my post grad Early Years Teacher status and landing a job as a Deputy Nursery Manager - Success. However these should not diminish the value of the daily and weekly successes. For me, that's managing to take my son to gymnastics, my daughter to our baby class, cooking meals every night. Weekly success for me would be sticking to TOMM (the organised mum method) to keep on top of my cleaning; I'm yet to achieve a full day let alone a full week or eight week cycle but every day I strive for it!

As a small aside, I came across an analogy the other day about striving for success. I'm going to paraphrase it as I cant recall it exactly but the gist of it was this; 'my dog is eight years old. Every morning he wakes up determined to catch a squirrel. He waits, he searches and he gives chase and to this day he has never caught one. Does this stop him believing in himself? Does it stop him waking up every day striving to catch a squirrel? No it does not. He believes in himself and his ability. And who are we to say he will never catch one?' I think this is a great image and one to remind us not to give up on ourselves or our drive to succeed.

I mentioned earlier about feeling under qualified to write about success. However the more I have thought about this and typed these words out the more empowered I have felt within myself. Breaking down success into daily and weekly successes, bigger and smaller successes, realising the true definition of success and not a media portrayal of success has embolden me.

I struggle a lot with my mental health and have done for many years; fourteen so far, well fourteen diagnosed years anyway. I have depression and anxiety; my journey is one of my greatest success stories. Aside from my husband and children! My journey is ongoing and ever evolving and on reflection, having said it is one of my successes it has made me acknowledge that success can also be in stages along the journey to achieving one goal. We have to celebrate and acknowledge the smaller successes on the road to the final goal. This can be applied in many ways especially for those of you with job and business goals. You want to start your own company? Celebrate the mini milestones along the way e.g. when you get your trademark through, when you sign off on policies, when you buy your first piece of equipment or hire your first member of staff, any of those are success on your way to success! It's all about how you look at it.

If we go back to the definition of success I provided earlier I think we would all be surprised at how successful we really are. Take a minute and write down who you are, what defines you and you will be surprised at how successful you are. But don't stop there, carry on striving for further success. Success isn't something that can be counted, it's a result of working towards or striving for something. It is something only you can define, it cannot be defined for you. Society will tell you what success is in on its own terms but true success lies within you. Maybe you want to be CEO of a company, that's ok. That is your goal and will (partly) define how successful you feel you are. Maybe you want to be mentally or physically well. Your goal is to be free from medication or find the correct level of medication and therapy for you and that will define how successful you feel in life. Whatever it is, make sure you are looking at success from the correct definition. By doing that you will be able to correctly determine YOUR success, not society's view of your success.

In closing, I hope the inner ramblings of my mind have been helpful to you. Trust in yourself, believe in yourself and most of all be kind to yourself.

Love and blessings,

Liz xx.

"Success doesn't come from what you do occasionally. It comes from what you do consistently"

MARIE FORLEO

Chapter 21

There Is Life After Childhood Sexual Abuse

Becca Bryant

Becca wants every woman to know that their voice can change the world. She is a dog obsessed home fragrance and décor specialist offering alternatives to candles and chemicals.

She also runs a support group for women who were sexually abused as children to help them see that there is life after childhood sexual abuse.

Her work doesn't stop there, she also runs a support group with fellow author, Edwina Clark, for Network Marketers who want to change the industry from being all about the sale to being about helping people

Instagram: @thebeccabryant
Facebook Group: Becca's Smelly Club
www.petsmellbegone.scentsy.co.uk

Facebook Group: Dear Little Girl
Facebook Group: MLM Hang Out

Do you remember those 'career tests' from School?

I always got given roles that are in the sports industry. Probably not a surprise as I was (at the time) an elite artistic gymnast.

However, there was a secret I was keeping, and I knew that I would never work in the industry for as long as the culture was as it was back then.

I was good at gymnastics, like really good. I had lots of power and was at one point British Number three at Tumbling.

Soaring through the sky, doing twists and turns was what I loved best.

But I got injured and my career hopes were dashed.

Gone.

No more gymnastics.

Until, I joined a local and low level club.

This was where my life changed and my journey began.

I was fourteen years of age and my coach sexually abused me. He didn't take long to groom me and I kept it a secret until I was in my late teens. I loved my sport. Now I hated it.

Teens were pretty tricky for me, but I managed to come out of School with eleven GCSE's, two A Levels and a AS Level (woodwork wasn't my finest choice!)

I was fortunate that I pretty much walked into a job after this. I breezed the interview and embarked on a fifteen year career within the local authority. I did a variety of roles while there; Call Handler, Project Assistant, PA and finally I became a Family Worker. I did this because I was going to change the world! I was going to be the one to save ALL children from abuse…… that didn't work out! I realised that it wasn't the children who needed 'saving' it was the adults who needed educating!

It was while being a Family Worker that I suffered a serious decline in my mental health and one day it just clicked…… Big Walkies.

I'd grown up with dogs and they were quite literally my life savers.

I set up a dog walking community group and used social media to spread the word.... Big Walkies grew and grew and grew!

We were helping so many people.

It didn't matter where you lived, what job you had (or didn't have), what you looked like – you just had to love dogs! And we all did!

From there I decided, after realising that I could not afford rent on my Local Authority income, that I set up my own company! Pet Staycation...... a service where I would stay in people's homes with their pets for a fee.

I learnt so much during that time! Firstly – charge what you are worth, not £10 a night because people WILL take advantage of you! Secondly – tax is confusing, if you can – get a professional to do it for you! Thirdly – it broke my heart to be away from my own dogs.

I stumbled across a network marketing company by pure accident. I joined on a whim (mainly to steal the kit) and WOW now my life was really going to change!

I did not expect anything from this opportunity. Nothing, at all.

What I did find was an industry where I could be ME! 100% me, sharing products I loved that were safe for dogs and humans alike AND make money AND be at home with my dogs AND fit it around my new day job for a local charity.

It was AMAZING! Hard work.... But amazing!

I have met the most incredible people; I have received the most amazing training and I've become the woman I was always supposed to be.

Confident.

I now support a team of thirty to do the same as I do, just in their way with them being unashamedly themselves.

I also founded and now co-run a support group for over one thousand four hundred Network Marketers from around the globe! The MLM Hang Out aims to support Network Marketers to be unashamedly them and not the carbon 'copy and paste' rubbish you see around!

With the support of a movement, Mums In Business International I have also set up a support group for women (who like me) were sexually abused as children. Dear Little Girl: There Is Life

After Sexual Abuse unites those who feel alone. We support each other navigate life. We celebrate and uplift each other; every, single, day.

I hope that my Network Marketing business (Pet Smell Be Gone) continues to thrive and that I can reach and support as many people as possible.

This isn't the end of my story, it's just the beginning.

If you are reading this and have been through the mill……. Do not give up! There is life after trauma. I am proof of this.

"I never thought of myself as a female engineer, or founder, or a woman in tech. I just think of myself as someone who is passionate"

LEAH BUSQUE

Chapter 22

Just Start Somewhere

Antonia Gough

Kindness begun with the understanding that we all struggle, now Antonia is changing the way people think about charity and giving back.

Making Kindness cool and creating a movement. Homeless House is a forever growing family who are changing lives one day at a time and preventing homelessness in our youths.

Instagram: @_homelesshouse

www.homelesshouse.co.uk

As I sit to write this, I am already doubting whether I want to share my journey as I am such a private person, however I continue and start to reflect on my past only I wonder where to start. I guess back at the beginning would be the best place.

As a child, I was one of six children to two beautiful hardworking parents from Liverpool. My dad working in a glass factory for over thirty years before his retirement with a strong woman for my mum who at one time collectively held three cleaning jobs, to ensure we had what we required to always have food on the table, clean clothes on our backs and holidays. My parents worked extremely hard and whilst they did so being the second oldest (oldest girl) I took the role of ensuring my younger brothers and sisters ate breakfast and were dressed in time for mum to come home from her first job and take them to school. Weekends we had chores to complete before we had fun. The dreaded cleaning the stairs with a wire brush, I hated that task! With every stroke I knew I was lightening the load for my parents.

The rest of my childhood weekends were filled with shopping with mum rummaging in our local charity shops (Mum still loves a bargain to this day) and long walks picking berries with my brother and sisters or apples for my mum to bake in a pie, or on the motorbike with dad over the local woodland. The holidays in a camper van with my uncle and the rest of my family to the holidays abroad all eight of us! I have no idea how my parents managed to juggle us all and allow us to have so many happy memories, for those I will be forever grateful.

Age thirteen I started church and also got my first job, I remember being so excited to go into a dirty, cold garage attached to the home of our local milkman, who lived in the street behind my home. What seemed like hundred of sacks of potatoes and a little scale with a 5 Kilo weight I set out to remove the potatoes from the sacks into plastic bags ensuring I met the 5KG balance in which he had taught me. I remember at the end of the week holding the first brown envelope, my payment within. That feeling tripped a switch which set my mindset for the next twenty-five years.

By the age of fourteen I continued to balance that little rusty scale, only now I was balancing my time with school, the love of helping my parents with my siblings, a paper round (which ended quickly I was soon worked out that the £10 something to walk around in the rain with a heavy sack on my still growing shoulders was not worth it). I traded this for another brand-new job. It was in a paper shop every Saturday. I remember feeling nervous however I soon picked up the ropes and was at fifteen on my own on weekends and now after school twice a week. I loved the feeling of running something on my own and I remained there till I was sixteen along with church.

Over the next seven years I had a few jobs my first on leaving soon, in the legal and Civic department of our local town hall. It was not high level as it sounds (chuckling to myself as I recall). It was a typing and post room. This is where I realised that lying in an interview was not the best idea. I had told my now boss I could type, I could but not at speed. I mean in my day there was no fast finger texting practice. What seemed like an angel took me under her wing. This lady was in her thirties very vibrant and very kind. This was my first experience in a business arrangement with the outcome being that she took a lot of my work whilst I enrolled at night school in a college to complete a typing course. Now I could type but I was bored so I booked to go onto my first girls' holiday to Spain at seventeen.

It was whilst I was there that I realised there was more to the world and on my return not long after I left. I guess the feeling of running something rather than a clocking system running me was too much. By the age of nineteen and now a Supervisor in Quality Control I had left home and bought my first house still close to my family. The role gave me more responsibility, I was walking into a business with myself being the only female. It was here that I was to grow in confidence, I found my voice. I have such fond memories of this place. By the age of thirty-three I had met a man whom I was to share the next eleven years and daughter with.

During this time, I began researching those who had been there before, Tesla, Einstein, looking at more than their work, transcripts. This led me on to looking into universal law, what they believed was possible. Quantum physics which I still have not got my head around. However, it took me back to church, only this time a spiritual church. I went to a few meetings and soon left as my gut feeling did not match what they believed. One thing I did believe was anything was possible. I began to really visualise working for myself.

By twenty-four I had left my much-loved job in QC and about to fuel the fire of being my own boss that had been burning within me since I was sixteen. We purchased a shop and continued within that business for twenty-four months during which my daughter was born and a further food truck implemented into our goals. On selling our business and making a great profit, I knew we had the skill set to buy, build up and sell. This is what we continued to do within a further four businesses, until a fifth business choice later cost us everything. I remember being more upset at myself for not standing up and pushing back for what it is I had wanted. This mistake cost me greatly and this was a turning point in my life which brings me to present day.

Those days and the immediate years to follow taught me more than I could ever have imagined. I had worked so hard, whilst my friends had memories I had worked three hundred and sixty five days a year during my self-employed period, missed the girly holidays and wild young nights out and now found myself in a position where I was a single mum starting over. Feeling exhausted and lost I went through so many emotions and more changes occurred over the next few years and it was a time in which the next trip was switched.

Even though I had little money, I remember (like it was only yesterday) pushing my daughter's pram down the street, it was cold and dark so must have been winter time, she was singing, and I recall us being the happiest. I knew there where people much worse off, this led me to start my giving back journey. It started with Operation Shoebox, I gathered hundreds of shoe boxes (care packages) which were shipped out to our service men and women overseas, this was made possible by my immediate community via a local newspaper reporter picking this up and running with a story. My giving back continued with the shoeboxes and helping the homeless and eventually I took another job within Vimto working in the Technical department at head office in Newton Le Willows for the wonderful Marnie Millard. I went to the interview thinking this is short term, until I can start my own thing again and having said this in my interview, I did not expect to be given a start. Little did I realise this would be my family for a further four years. Vimto will always hold a special place in my heart. I could breathe and be myself again, implementing changes, taking control, really enjoying my work. Only there was nothing that could put out that feeling that I needed to continue to make a difference only with my own vision and on my own terms.

It was in 2019 I knew my passion was to help others, giving back by donations was simply not enough. Placing a band aid for this to be torn away to replace this again and watch the pattern repeat was frustrating. For the first time in my life I felt trapped. In a job that I enjoyed but was no longer passionate about. I really struggled with my own thoughts for quite some time, looking for the right place to start. Putting the wheels in motion to put back on the brakes in times of doubt. It was a real challenge as everything I had ever done had happened to me not that I had made it happen. Or so I thought.

It was during a work day at my desk whilst listening to podcast (which I did most days) which talked of "Just start somewhere" and reminded me of my first interview of accepting a position I could not do with the belief that I would figure it out as I go. With that I took to Instagram and slowly started to build a page. It has now been twelve months. I continued to work on the fire that built in my gut for now over twenty years only my aim was not to have lots but to give lots to communities that have nothing. Six months into a dream of helping others still with no plan, I worked hard finishing my full time job at 4pm to arrive home, do dinner, spend time with my daughter and work till the early hours on Homeless House. This continued with the weekends allowing me more time, this excited me. With every comment, like and person who joined me on wanting to give back. We became a Family. Homeless House was really happening.

In October of this year I was fortunate to meet a man who also believed in me. Not only did he have belief but a wonderful heart. After many conversations of what I had seen, what I believed could make a difference with a presentation of my vision, I was offered the chance to leave my position at Vimto and work on Homeless House to continue giving back. Even though this is what I had wanted I still took to my CEO 'Marnie' at Vimto and we had a conversation. I will not go into what Marnie and I spoke of however she reminded me of what I had set out to achieve and spoken of the words back to me in which I said moments earlier in that "I was very lucky". I remember leaving her glass office, looking around and sitting back at my desk with mixed emotions, sadness as I knew I was leaving and nervously excited of what was to come. With the overriding feeling of being very blessed. The next day I spoke to my boss and advised him of my notice. Some weeks later I left the building for the very last time.

It has since been six months within this time we have gained the support of some amazing individuals and business. Times of me and my sister sitting, throwing thoughts on ideas, travelling to places to make it work, travelling back with her at my side, dancing and smiling with the outcome. False promises, tears, sitting on cold pavements listening to stories and a whole load of happy moments. A call from an unexpected person when you are ready to throw in the towel. Feelings of being alone and what to do now. Then a global pandemic within the first ten weeks of moving into my new Manchester based office. Had I have known this would I have left Vimto? Hell no! It would have been I will do it some day. I have had to learn fast and I will be learning for a long time to come, which excites me. I never stop learning and do not believe we should. I have had to grow in patience, Lord knows I have never had any and to be less controlling (which my Vimto colleagues will probably not believe that this has changed Ha-ha). I also recognise that the years I have grown through have brought me to this moment. It is a place which is new on paper but old to my heart. I feel like I am home.

I will now be working on continuing to make kindness cool, to show our younger generations that our homeless extended family once had a position within employment, a family, a life free from hunger with hope. That I was in a position that if not for a loving family and friends could have turned out so differently. I want to ensure that I finish what I set out to do and for as many as I can, to remove the band aid for the very last time.

My final thoughts to you if are just leaving school, Uni and feel lost. That is okay, do not worry none of us really had a clue what we were doing anyway and many of us still do not know, it always works out. If you have something niggling and it will not go away yet you do not know where to start "Just start somewhere". I hope if nothing else I hope that me sharing a piece of my journey so far this has inspired just one person, to really believe that, if you believe you can! You Will!

Be Blessed everyone,

Antonia

"If you want to be successful, be unique."

NATALIE MASSANET

Chapter 23

Cocktails, Children & Cleaning

Victoria Rothwell

Being present as both mummy and a multi 6 figure business owner.
Victoria wants mums out there to know that they can build a successful multi 6 or 7 figure business and still be there on the school run, be sat around the dinner table every evening with their children, be the one who does bath and bedtime.

BE PRESENT
Be present in both your business and as mummy to your children.
The business blueprint she has nurtured and developed offers exactly this and Victoria is very passionate about supporting women and helping them grow and feel confident as a business owner.

www.thebeautifulmethod.co.uk

Facebook: @thebeautifulmethodHQ. @thebeautifulmethodChester
Instagram: @thebeautifulmethod

Ever since I was a little girl I always dreamt of owning my own business, but I can honestly say that housekeeping was never part of that dream. In fact, like most little girls my dreams involved something a lot more glamorous like fashion or advertising. Think catwalks, cocktails and travelling the world, they definitely didn't feature a mop and bucket that's for sure.

Growing up my dad always told us that I could pick my own GCSEs, A-level and degree subjects as they would shape our future, not his. Once these things were complete we could do as we liked as his jobs as a parent and educator were done.

I have always loved art and creative subjects which lead me to undertake a degree in fashion and textiles, and I loved every minute of it.... And I was still working towards my childhood dream of glamour and catwalks.

Upon finishing my degree it took me two years to get my first job in fashion, but I was not giving up and I was determined to 'make it'. This job was worth the wait, I absolutely loved it. The meetings with designers, suppliers and high-street stores were a dream come true. I would spend half of my week in London playing on Oxford Street including a weekly trip to Liberty and the other half travelling the world including some amazing party nights in Hong Kong. I was in my element, I loved my job and everything it entailed, but there was still something missing. As much as I loved my job it wasn't MY business. I still felt the need to fulfil my childhood ambition of running my own company.

In the midst of my glamorous fashion lifestyle, in 2008 I met Jonathon, the man of my dreams and it changed everything. We bought our first home, got married and it was amazing, it still is all these years later. Amongst the bliss of a job I loved and a wonderful relationship, we decided to start a family. And that is when my world started to fall apart.

The pregnancy itself was ok apart from the fact that my bump was enormous and I had to give up work earlier than planned, but as I went into labour in late June of 2012 things took an unexpected turn. My labour which lasted for two days concluded in a birth which I can only describe as horrendous. Both my son and I very nearly didn't make it; my sister describes it as "like a scene from casualty". The doctors and midwives rushed me through to theatre pumping fluids into my body to give me and my son the best chance of survival.

Thankfully I have no vivid memories of this moment, but I do remember most of what happened afterwards. The memory of being very ill in a hospital bed and phoning my husband in the dead of night crying and begging him to come and take me home isn't easily forgotten. Neither is being forced to try and breastfeed even though I was lying in bed with sepsis, after emergency surgery unable to move. I will never forget lying in a hospital bed listening to my baby scream whilst being unable to get out of bed to pick him up. Then in she walked...

I can't remember her name, and to be honest I am not even sure if she was real. What I do remember is a pair of dark blue glasses, bleached blonde hair and a very strong smell of cigarettes. She was a midwife and she arrived at the exact moment that my son and I needed her. Her first words were "this is fucking ridiculous, a fed baby is what's best; not whether its breast or bottle". She gave me three mini bottles of formula and my little boy who was born weighing 9lb 6oz guzzled all three bottles.

I spent the next twelve weeks in and out of the hospital as I wasn't getting any better and my body wasn't healing. I couldn't believe my ears when I heard the words 'I think we need to scan you, Mrs Rothwell, to check nothing has been left inside".... Are you fucking kidding me!

Fast forward to six months after my son was born and I was unsurprisingly diagnosed with severe PND and anxiety. It was a horrible time and if it wasn't for my husband and my family I am not sure I would have made it through. I had a lot of therapy and thought I was ok, so when my son was 18months old I went back to work.

But, I quickly found out that things just weren't the same, I wasn't the same. Being away from home and having a family just didn't work for us anymore, so I quit. But never content to stand still this is when my childhood dream of running my own business came back into my mind and I started my first business Gobi Knitwear shortly afterwards.

Gobi was a small label selling cashmere pieces through my website and at winter fairs. Everything was going swimmingly, my new business was really working, the business was building and I was getting a nice following. However, I'm never one to stand still so it was then that I turned to my hubby and said... "hey fancy having another baby"?

I was never sure if I wanted another baby, but what I did know is that I didn't want my son to be an only child, and I told myself that this time would be different and I would make sure I had full control over my labour.

So, with baby number two decided on we tried to get pregnant, but nothing happened. So, on New Year's Eve 2014 we decided that getting pregnant clearly wasn't working and it was 'just meant to be' the three of us - and that was good enough.

But like all things in life, it wasn't that simple. On New Years Day 2015 with the decision to stop trying and enjoy my family of three at the front of my mind, I woke up feeling odd. My first thought was that I had a hangover as we had really enjoyed the night before, but something made me take a pregnancy test anyway and, low and behold the two lines appeared - boom we were pregnant.

A few weeks later I started to bleed and again I accepted the fact that adding more children to our family was just not meant to be. So, I called my mum and she made me go the doctors who then sent me for a scan. Off we went to the hospital expecting to be told that I'd had a miscarriage. I was lying on the bed and the sonographer was asking me lots of questions. How have you been feeling? Really, really tired? Have you been feeling sick? All the while my mind is shouting why are you asking me these questions I've had a miscarriage!

I could not have been more wrong... Its TWINS...WHAT????

I started laughing, I couldn't help it, what are the odds? I then turned to Jonathon to find him sitting on the floor crying. We got ourselves together and once we were outside the first thing he said to me was... Do you know how expensive that is going to be?

The pregnancy was fine, as was the birth this time and our twin daughters arrived in late summer 2015. I felt ok, so I carried on working, gearing up to my busiest time of year. I asked my mum for help and she was there when I needed her. Between them, my parents held the fort at the weekend with my three-year-old son and three-month-old twins whilst I did one of the biggest shows of the year. It was brilliant, the fair was a huge success and I had my best sales to date.

Then I arrived home... although they love my children dearly my parents said it was too much to look after three small children on their own and they just couldn't do it any more, (they were in their late 60's so it was a big ask).

So, with huge sadness, but the best interests of my family at heart I had no choice but to fold the business. Closing my business had a massive effect on my mental health, I felt devastated all over again and when the twins were 6 months old I was diagnosed with severe PND and anxiety. It was during my second round of therapy that we discovered that I still hadn't processed the trauma of giving birth to my son and the stress of the six months since the twins were born had triggered it all again.

So, I took the time I needed to deal with the trauma I had suffered, the effect it was having not just on me but my family too. It was tough, on everyone, especially my son who was old enough to actually see it this time, and that broke my heart. But I struggled through and made sure I healed properly so that my son and I didn't have to go through any more trauma. As a three-year-old he had experienced too much already. I put myself back together so I could be me again. I realised that I couldn't be the mum my children needed or the fun-loving wife again until I was ok. Not just alright, not just about holding on, but fully back to the me that existed before June 2012.

With months of therapy and a much happier head on my shoulders, I started looking for a new career. You see I love my kids to bits but I'm just not made to be a stay at home mum, I needed something for me. I also knew that with my husband and me out a lot more, we were going to need some help around the house. I wanted to make the most of the time I wasn't at work spending time with my children making memories together, not catching up on housework.

So. I started looking around for some domestic help, cleaning, ironing general family mess management. But, I soon found that I couldn't find one that used eco-products (we are in the country with a septic tank, so no bleach allowed) that could do everything I needed them to do and was reliable.

I tried a few, and they all started out great but then their standards would begin to slip or they just didn't turn up, and it drove me mad. But it also put an idea in my head. I couldn't be the only person in the world that was sick of being let down by their domestic services?

With the seed of this idea growing, I set about doing some research and discovered that I definitely wasn't. There was a real gap in the market for good, eco-friendly and reliable domestic help. And this is how by complete accident (like all good ideas) that I decided to develop The Beautiful Method.

I started working on the business in September 2016, making sure that I got everything right. I wanted to take the time to create a service that covered everything a busy working mum needed. Preparation is everything.

With everything in place, I launched The Beautiful Method Housekeeping Services in March 2017.

Was I mad? Err, yes! With eighteen-month-old twins and four-year-old son at home I was very busy, but I knew I could do it and what's more, I knew the service was needed by other families. Not just families who needed our services but other parents who needed flexible and secure jobs so they could get back to work whilst spending time with their family. It was always my intention right from the start to build a business that cares.

The business that I started to give time to my family has gone from strength to strength and now gives time to lots of other families, not just the ones who use our services but the many amazing parents who work for us.

This business that started as a lightbulb moment has surpassed all of my expectations in two short years. We have client enquiries every day and due to the demand from other towns and cities in the UK this year I launched The Beautiful Method Franchising Group.

By franchising, I can offer other parents a tried and tested business model which really works, operations and full support from me and my amazing team.

My business model is certainly family-friendly, it has to be as I need it to work for me, and my family. I need (not want) to fulfil my drive and ambition but I also want to be there for my children. I want to be the one who drops them off and picks them up from school, I'm there at every bath and bedtime. I don't want to miss a thing because I know that one day soon they will be too cool to hang out with mummy.

Don't get me wrong my kids drive me nuts and let me tell you we are not the perfect family, but I chose to be a mum and I love being it, but I also choose to be me!

I have always wanted to build my own business, I just had to adapt my dream to suit my new life as a mummy, and I know there are other parents out there who would love this opportunity too.
I am passionate about making this amazing business opportunity available to other parents across the UK who are not 'just' mummy and daddy but are also capable, driven and ambitious women and men. I understand more than anyone the need to be a hands-on parent whilst also running a business that makes our quality of life possible.

The Housekeeping business I have built over the last three years is now a multi six figure business and it is this model that is now available to other women. I'm offering them their own business with the help and support of the TBM brand.

It really is a ready made business in a box (and if you don't fancy yourself as the next Mrs Hinch, don't worry, as a franchisee there is no cleaning involved). I have done all of the development, taken all of the risks, made all the mistakes to get it just right and ready to offer it to other entrepreneurial-minded parents. We are there for our franchisees every day throughout their business journey, they get full access to our operations, HR, Health and Safety, CRM system, their own website, full marketing launch and most importantly the support and guidance from me and my team.

We can all have the gift of time and be present for our families. I truly believe that every parent has the right to a secure and flexible role so that they can be present as a parent and do a job that they love, without judgement, or discrimination. We are a really supportive group of women and we support all of our clients, franchisees and team members whether they are head office, housekeeping or one of the many families we help.

Throughout the ups and downs of birth-trauma, unexpected twins, a shit load of therapy and two businesses, the main thing I've learnt is that happiness lies in the people that you surround yourself with. My incredible husband, kids, friends and family got me through a really hard time in my life. The amazing women I have met since creating The Beautiful Method have made this incredible business what it is today. I genuinely want as many women as possible to have the opportunities that my team and I have created.

You can be in business for yourself, but you don't need to be by yourself.

Your Turn

LIONESS

What are your goals?

it is important to have goals because it gives you long term vision and short term motivation. It allows you to make decisions to work towards achieving your goals.

3 months:

6 months:

1 year:

Www.lionesspride.co.uk

LIONESS

Today I am thankful for:

We can get so wrapped up in everyday life and the struggles and triumphs we sometimes forget to be thankful. maybe you are thankful your family are in good health? Or your business has made a good profit this week? Think of three things.

Www.lionesspride.co.uk

LIONESS

Three Reasons

Your three reasons for starting this career.

LIONESS

Time to BE

- Be Lucky
Some people appear to be lucky but are just more likely to be putting themselves out there. Making connections and working on their business.

-Be Giving
Good things happen to those who give and being a kind, helpful person. Help others and in return they will help you.

-Be Prepared to Grow
While running your business it will grow and develop in ways you cannot plan. Believe you can get better and achieve more.

-Be a Visionary
Runners jump hurdles when running a race. Your vision CAN be a reality but be prepared to put in the effort.

- Be a Student
Life is always a learning curve but especially in terms of business. All the things that go wrong and fail are just opportunities to bounce back.

You win some you LEARN some.

Www.lionesspride.co.uk

LIONESS

Failure

Do <u>NOT</u> get hung up
Do not get hung up your failures.
Accept things didn't go to plan, move on, learn and adapt.

Do <u>NOT</u> be scared
Get out there, don't be scared of failure.

"As human beings we are not naturally afraid of looking stupid or failing we get educated into it" Steli Effi

<u>MOST</u> things fail
You re-adjust, learn from the experience and bounce back stronger and better.

Www.lionesspride.co.uk

LIONESS

Three Goals

Three things I am going to achieve before the end of the day.

Www.lionesspride.co.uk

LIONESS

Three Goals

Three things I am going to achieve before the end of the month:

Www.lionesspride.co.uk

LIONESS

Daily Practices
Whether it is a routine or getting up and having a shower. Having a cup of tea or maybe meditating, business related things such as doing a social media post at breakfast. Or a blog post at lunch time.

Plan
Start everyday with a plan.
What are you going to do today?
What are your MUSTS are things that need doing but if they don't today it's fine.
Are they time sensitive? Do you have to have an e-mail sent out before lunchtime?
Do you need to go to the post office before it closes?

Time Boundaries
Don't spend all day on the same task (unless you are getting somewhere with it)
Spending time on something doesn't mean it's productive. A break from it is sometimes needed. Don't be afraid to do this.
Walk away or work on something else.

Www.lionesspride.co.uk

LIONESS

What have you done today to make you feel proud?

Role Model
You are showing your children how to believe in ourselves, and how to be a success. Your children are always watching and they want you to be happy and successful. You are being a strong female role model for them to look up to and model.

Job satisfaction
Knowing that all your hard work pays off is a huge amount of satisfaction. You get out what you put in so work hard to reap the rewards. That your product or service is loved by so many people who want to tell the world about it, really is an amazing feeling.

Www.lionesspride.co.uk

LIONESS

Looking After You

Positive mental attitude is a contributing factor of success.

By focussing on positive thoughts throughout the day and any negative situations seeing the positive can give you a whole new view of life. It has also been linked to lower risk of depression and other mental health problems.

Triggers

Triggers is usually used in a negative term but we are going to use it in a positive way. By knowing what triggers happy behaviour and feeling we can control our mood.

My husband walks the dog when he gets in from work too destress. Some people have a bath, take a walk, go to the gym or listen to music.

Www.lionesspride.co.uk

LIONESS

Belief
Believe you can do it, bounce back from failures and bumps in the road.

Think Ahead
Like in chess you think of the three moves ahead. Plan your business, plan your marketing and think if I do A it will lead to B then C.

Big and Small
Celebrate all your wins no matter how big or small.

Avoid Stagnation
Keep fresh, keep adapting, keep learning. See what is the current trend and use this to your advantage.

Gut Instinct
Confidence in your instincts is a critical component of business success. **T**here are a variety of scenarios in when empirical evidence is unavailable or inconclusive.

Www.lionesspride.co.uk

LIONESS

Self - Employed & Motherhood

Freedom
Being a mum means we want to take our kids to school, we want to be there for the nativity play and for everything for our kids. Being self-employed gives us the freedom to do this.

Flexibility
If our child is ill or we are or they have an inset day we don't have to worry about childcare. We don't have to ask our boss for permission to be off. We set our own diary.

Holidays
We can have any holidays we like when we like, no need to ask permission to have some time off during the six weeks holiday. You decide when and when you do not work.

Www.lionesspride.co.uk

LIONESS

Name three things your brand stands for:
(e.g. luxury or necessity, family orientated or business orientated etc)

Www.lionesspride.co.uk

LIONESS

Mindset Matters

- Determination
It won't be easy, it will be rocky but you can do it, you will have off days but sleep them off and come back the next day stronger.

- Patience

It won't come straight away, be kind to yourself, believe in yourself. It can take years to start making a profit. It will be worth it - trust me.

- Pro-Active
Show people this is what you do, this is how you do it. Be working on your business whenever you can to take it to the next level.

Www.lionesspride.co.uk

LIONESS

Make Connections

A part of running a business is networking with other people and business owners. You never know where a new connection will lead you.
If you share the same clientele you can work together to share each others posts. And inform your customers about one another.

Get Out There

I know this can seem a hard one, if you are introverted but there are many ways to do this. You can have the most amazing product/service in the world but if nobody knows about it you will not get any sales. If you sell a product and can have a stall at an event this is a great opportunity for you. If you sell a product maybe send it to influencers/reviewers. If you have a service you can also offer this to people in terms of a competition so you can get reviews to build up your business page.

Www.lionesspride.co.uk

LIONESS

Long Term Goals

This could be to own your own house, pay off your debts, get married etc. These are what your business will achieve in the long term.

LIONESS

Three things that make you unique

Think deeply about what is going to make you stand out from the competition. What do you do differently to your competitors?

Www.lionesspride.co.uk

LIONESS

Why

Your "why" is what is going to keep you focussed. What is your "why" for you running your business. Maybe it is to provide financial security for your children. Maybe you are saving money for a mortgage or something else. You could even type up and print your "why" off and stick it on your fridge. Whenever you hit a low read your "why".

Www.lionesspride.co.uk

LIONESS

Be Reliable
- With delivery times with your clients so they know exactly how you run your business.
- If you have a store make sure it has regular opening hours that you commit.

Be Trustworthy
- With customer details keep them safe, GDPR means you legally have to keep any personal details stored securely.
- If a client messages you those messages are private between you and the client.

Be Consistent
- Product/Service quality, people will come to you and use you again and again as long as you are consistent.

Www.lionesspride.co.uk

LIONESS

Success

Success means different things to different people. it is very hard to compare one person's success to another. For some it is financial security, for others it is family situations. Write down what success means to you.

Www.lionesspride.co.uk

Printed by Amazon Italia Logistica S.r.l.
Torrazza Piemonte (TO), Italy